Gender, Monitoring
and Learning

Praise for this book

'This publication is very timely as it provides a well-articulated framework for integrating gender equality and women's empowerment into development evaluation. The different chapters help to "square the circle" by addressing all of the methodological, political, organizational and ideological factors that affect the design and implementation of an effective gender-responsive evaluation strategy. It combines a review of gender-responsive tools and techniques, and reviews of different evaluation approaches that development agencies are currently using, with detailed case studies documenting experiences using different evaluation approaches. The publication will prove useful both to readers concerned with gender-responsive evaluation, as well as to those who are concerned with broader issues of how to improve the general practice of development evaluation.'

Michael Bamberger, independent development evaluation consultant

Gender, Monitoring, Evaluation and Learning

Edited by
Caroline Sweetman and Kimberly Bowman

PRACTICAL ACTION
Publishing

Practical Action Publishing Ltd
The Schumacher Centre,
Bourton on Dunsmore, Rugby,
Warwickshire, CV23 9QZ, UK
www.practicalactionpublishing.org

A catalogue record for this book is available from the British Library.
A catalogue record for this book has been requested from the Library of Congress.

ISBN 978-1-78853-002-6 hardback
ISBN 978-1-78853-003-3 paperback
ISBN 978-1-78044-704-9 library pdf
ISBN 978-1-78044-710-0 ebook

Citation: Sweetman, C. and Bowman, K. (eds) (2017) *Gender, Monitoring, Evaluation and Learning*, Rugby, UK: Practical Action Publishing and Oxford: Oxfam GB, <http://dx.doi.org/10.3362/9781780447049>.

Since 1974, Practical Action Publishing has published and disseminated books and information in support of international development work throughout the world. Practical Action Publishing is a trading name of Practical Action Publishing Ltd (Company Reg. No. 1159018), the wholly owned publishing company of Practical Action. Practical Action Publishing trades only in support of its parent charity objectives and any profits are covenanted back to Practical Action (Charity Reg. No. 247257, Group VAT Registration No. 880 9924 76).

Oxfam is a registered charity in England and Wales (no 202918) and Scotland (SC 039042). Oxfam GB is a member of Oxfam International.

Oxfam GB,
Oxfam House, John Smith Drive,
Oxford, OX4 2JY, UK
www.oxfam.org.uk

Cover photo credit: Development Impact Evaluation, World Bank,
Practical Action Publishing photo library, Rugby
Printed in the United Kingdom

FSC

Contents

http://dx.doi.org/10.3362/9781780447049.000

CHAPTER 1

Introduction to gender, monitoring, evaluation and learning

Kimberly Bowman and Caroline Sweetman

Abstract

This chapter provides an overview of gender, monitoring, evaluation and learning (MEL), and introduces the chapters that follow. It argues that MEL is a powerful tool for feminists to use to chart the impact of development policies and programming on women's rights and gender equality. Strong MEL practice can help to render policymakers, practitioners and researchers more accountable to the individuals and groups they aim to support, as well as accountable to the funders and supporters of that work.

Keywords: monitoring, evaluation, learning, gender equality, women's rights

Introduction

In recent years, increasing commitment to gender equality and women's rights in development has sparked interest in gender-sensitive and gender-responsive methods of development evaluation. This book offers a unique opportunity to share different experiences of monitoring, evaluating and learning about the effect of development and humanitarian work on women's empowerment and gender equality. It presents the collected articles published in a recent issue of the journal, *Gender & Development*.

On the face of it, Monitoring, Evaluation, and learning (MEL), may seem to be a somewhat dry, technical topic. Yet it is in fact profoundly political. We would even suggest that a good MEL system is an activist's best friend! MEL provides feminists with the means to explore the gendered impact of programmes and projects on all affected by them. To what extent have development programmes supported women in their daily lives, and in their struggles for equality and justice? Strong MEL practice can help to render policymakers, practitioners and researchers more accountable to the individuals and groups they aim to support, as well as accountable to the funders and supporters of that work.

The chapters in this book capture the knowledge of a range of development practitioners and women's rights activists. They situate their analysis of real experiences of MEL in the context of the role it plays in driving forward

http://dx.doi.org/10.3362/9781780447049.001

real change for those living in poverty in the global South. The primary lens used usually involves unpicking differential experiences of men and women (females and males) – though we note that many encounter challenging and complex inequalities stemming from the intersection of identities, including race, class, age, sexuality and gender identity, age, caste, and (dis)ability. Most (though not all) of the contributors to this collection are staff members in development organisations of different kinds. Others make their living as independent consultants. Authors are drawn from many different kinds of organisation, and come from both the global South and North. All have tried to share their experience accessibly, making what is often very complex and technical material as clear as possible to non-MEL specialists.

In this brief Introduction, we provide some context, offering a brief account of the ways research into the impact of development interventions on women and girls has shaped gender and development policy and practice as we see it today. If MEL approaches are underpinned by a strong gender analysis and feminist commitment to change, they can be a huge help in the wider process of integrating gender equality and women's rights into development organisations. We go on to introduce the chapters, and highlight some of the successes, insights, challenges and dilemmas they share.

Gender and development (GAD) and MEL: the evolution of a field

Monitoring, evaluation and learning is in the DNA of gender and development (GAD) as a field of activism and enquiry. GAD's story began with feminist researchers mapping – that is, informally evaluating – the impact on women, and development, of mistaken understandings of women's role in economic development in the global South. New thinking about gender identity, roles and relations produced a powerful account of the marginalization of half of the human race: to be seen as 'female' was a disadvantage in patriarchal societies, and the existence of individuals, groups and societies that differed from this norm was rendered invisible from historical accounts. Early studies pointed up the negative impact of development projects founded on mistaken top-down notions about gender relations and roles in the global South (Boserup 1971). These studies highlighted cultural diversity in gender relations, but also some extraordinary similarities between societies thousands of miles apart. Endemic poverty, violence and abuse among women and girls was the norm in societies worldwide, and gender inequality needed action at all levels, from local to global (see, for example, Young, Wolkowitz and McCullagh 1981).

Women in development (WID) programmes were launched to respond to these insights, and subsequent feminist research, monitoring and evaluation assessed the progress – and motivations – of development projects focusing on women. They were found wanting. Feminist anthropologists, economists and post-colonial writers in the global South and North critiqued WID agendas for failure to move beyond a focus on economic development along Western lines. This critique called for a radical transformation of the world order to challenge complex inequalities arising from gender, race and class (Sen and Grown 1987). This needed more than a WID project supporting women's livelihoods; it meant supporting women's collective action to further their interests as a marginalised group, supporting them to secure resources (not only income, but also assets and property denied to them, including land), and promoting their participation in decision-making at all levels of society (Kabeer 1994). It would involve transforming institutions – including governments and development organisations of all kinds – whose cultures were founded in bias against women (Elson 1995). In the wake of the UN Fourth World Conference on Women in 1995 in Beijing, the drive to integrate gender analysis into all aspects of development spurred governments and others on to 'mainstream gender' into systems and procedures, including monitoring and evaluation.

Parallel to the development of GAD as a field of activism and enquiry, and the agenda of gender mainstreaming, MEL established itself as a specialist discipline and body of approaches in development organisations, and MEL units were established to develop organisation-wide systems and approaches, often in response to institutional donor demands. A number of gender-analysis tools and frameworks were designed in the lead-up to Beijing and in the years following. They aimed to systematise an approach which could be used in planning and for MEL. Gender-analysis frameworks were intended to be used by non-gender specialist staff and partner organisations. These aim to ensure projects and programmes are designed, implemented, monitored and evaluated systematically from a gender perspective. Frameworks typically analyse the gender division of labour, the extent of women's and men's workloads, gendered patterns of time-use, and potential for activities designed to alleviate household poverty. Some go further, to uncover data concerned with gender power relations in the households and communities involved in research (March, Smyth and Mukhopadhyay 1999).

In their chapter, Emily Hillenbrand and colleagues focus on the use of a gender analysis framework for MEL focusing on the Fish on Farms project in Cambodia. Naila Kabeer's Social Relations Approach was selected for this work because of its focus on power relations (as distinct from simpler tools which limit their focus to gendered roles and responsibilities), and its understanding of the role of social institutions in challenging or shoring up gender inequality. This is the only chapter which explores the use of a gender framework; all others focus on MEL approaches developed in response to the specific needs of particular programmes or projects, and are introduced below.

The current context: gendered MEL in an era of management efficiency

In 2017, gender inequality, feminism and MEL, are 'hot topics', debated in think tanks, among policy-makers, and in governments and development organisations of all kinds. Agenda 2030 and the Sustainable Development Goals have reaffirmed and strengthened the need to focus on complex inequalities, including gender equality, for poverty alleviation and human development worthy of the name. Gender equality and women's rights are now seen as a critical means – as well as an end – for achieving development. Gender issues have been mainstreamed into the SDGs as well as addressed specifically in the 'Gender Goal', SDG 5. Accompanying the new consensus around gender equality as a critical concern for development is an upwards trend in acknowledging the importance of good MEL in development. Monitoring and evaluation of development projects seems more of a priority than ever, in a world of shrinking support for development assistance in the global North, and complex crises facing both South and North. These realities are creating new challenges to development research, policy and practice. Resources available for government-funded social services and for independently-funded development initiatives fall far short of the demand for them, and governments and development organisations are keener than ever to use their resources as efficiently as possible.

In the context of pressure on funding for development work, 'organisations working for women's rights and gender equality are under growing pressure to demonstrate results' (Batliwala 2011a, 1). The same sense of needing to make resources work as hard as possible underpins the current 'discovery' of women's empowerment (and to a lesser extent, women's rights and gender equality) by mainstream development agencies, as well as similar recent focus on women's *economic* empowerment by private sector actors and government. Gender is currently seen as 'smart economics' (Chant and Sweetman 2012). This focus on efficiency and economic participation potentially limits development programming – and MEL – to focus on more short-term and proximate process or 'economic advancement' indicators for workers and female entrepreneurs, while failing to ask critical questions about power and agency. Srilatha Batliwala critiqued the instrumentalist adoption of the language of empowerment only a few years ago; she noted that 'Resources for women's rights work are no longer a matter of human rights or social justice but more pragmatic considerations of social returns on "investments"' (Batliwala 2011b, 1).

However, feminists working in MEL highlight its potential to be a positive force for change in the world today. Despite the pressure to 'simply' demonstrate attributable impact and efficiency in very short time frames, we need to step up to the challenge of using systematic inquiry to do more – to challenge inequalities and injustices. Economic inequalities, the effects of climate change and other environmental degradation are worsening as global wealth rises. Fragility, violence and conflict are growing in many contexts and these challenge ideas about how we bring about sustainable human-centred development. In this context we desperately need MEL systems that help us challenge naïve, inappropriate or simplistic 'answers' to complex problems rooted in inequalities and injustices. We should seek out methods that help identify and magnify the voices and perspectives of those most marginalized, so that development decision-makers are forced to consider questions of equality and social justice over the long term (and not simply 'outputs' or bland or short-term statements of 'return on investment') in judging the value created by their efforts.

The chapters included here aim to help gender and development practitioners to understand how to 'square the circle' and manage pressure to report on results, while drawing on women's own perceptions of their lives and gender power relations to highlight areas where economic empowerment cannot deliver the changes needed. Development organisations of all kinds should be looking for the best value for money, using analysis to understand the complex scope of the change needed and allocate their scarce resources (time, attention and money) to genuinely support women living in poverty. MEL can be used to help guide practitioners in taking decisions responsibly and well, by holding our own organisations to account, and contributing to knowledge which will provide a foundation for better work in future.

In this book, Paola Pereznieto and Georgia Taylor of the UK Overseas Development Institute demonstrate how this can happen. They present findings from a review of 70 evaluations of development interventions which aimed to support the economic empowerment of women and girls. Critically, this ODI study defines economic empowerment as a process whereby women and girls experience transformation in power, agency and economic advancement. By moving beyond the narrower understandings of economic empowerment as purely and simply concerned with income generation, this study is itself useful in stimulating debate and learning among the practitioners and policymakers who will use it.

Capturing complexity and questioning 'knowledge'

As suggested in the last section, gendered approaches to MEL emphasise the importance of seeking out women's and girls' own analyses of development and its impact on their lives. MEL can help to transform development and the world we live in by exploring and recording the experience and perceptions of women – in particular, women living in poverty – whose lives have in the past gone largely unrecorded, and whose experiences have remained outside the realm of what is conventionally seen as knowledge. Recent debates on 'responsible data' challenge MEL practitioners and organizations to ensure that their practices – including data collection, storage and use – are in line with values of transparency, openness and rights-based approaches (O'Donnell 2015). Feminist ideas about research, learning, and 'knowledge' are as many and diverse as feminists themselves (Brisolara 2014, 3), but offer insights for MEL from a gender perspective. MEL usually means adopting a positivist stance – that is, one which tries hard to uncover a 'truth', or at least, a substantiated hypothesis which can be offered as a best interpretation – making sure that this is based on data generated from a range of different perspectives, and from systematic and transparent processes. In such a data-rich age, recent initiatives linked to monitoring the SDGs remind us of the major 'gendered data gap', including huge disparities in foundational statistical information about the lives of women and girls. While many MEL practitioners recognize the limitations of gendered national statistics, the ambition towards inclusion in recognized evidence bases at this scale, is a positive one.

Feminist 'standpoint theory' stresses that our location ('standpoint') affects what we think about our lives and experiences, and values the knowledge of marginalised social groups. Feminist MEL seeks to ensure that questions asked and conclusions provided draw on multiple perspectives, systematically and transparently. In many cases, this will enable previously unvoiced perspectives to come to the fore – and may challenge the dominance of professional or expert 'researchers' mining the experience of grassroots women and girls whose own identity and location means their views are seldom, if ever, sought.

In their chapter on Oxfam GB's Women's Empowerment Effectiveness Reviews, David Bishop and Kimberly Bowman speak of the importance of listening to nuanced and individual assessments of the changes development makes to the lives of women. Balancing the books regarding the time and cost of involving women in 'meaningful participation' is a challenge, but this is essential in order to gain a true picture of the impact of an intervention.

Feminist empiricism is the theory that we can only 'know' 'that which we experience (and measure) through our senses' (Brisolara 2014, 6); that there is no such thing as 'objective', or neutral. For feminists, empirical research is the first step in understanding women's condition and position in different parts of the world, and this in turn can enable support to justice-seeking activism by women themselves and by development organizations, philanthropists and governments which support them. In MEL terms, what development interventions require is preliminary research and analysis, which enables the design of projects which help and support women (individually and collectively). MEL can be further used to support collective understanding (of a change, how it is experienced by different people, and how a system reactors to it), and challenge complex inequalities, including gender inequality, in their own ways and to their own timelines.

Development often involves working in partnership; feminist practitioners seek approaches to MEL that empower partner organizations, rather than simply extract data. The tools of systematic inquiry must be used to amplify the voices of the less powerful, and inform the direction of development programming. Doing MEL in a development organisation which seeks to challenge unequal power, reduce economic and political inequality and support a changed global order which takes into account the interests of the poorest in our societies is a massive challenge. Women's rights activists call for a more genuine commitment to making MEL a learning partnership rather than 'mining' for facts or putting partner organisations through a performance test, and for a balance between quantitative and qualitative techniques and a use of multiple methods, gender analysis tools and frameworks. They also call for approaches which assess development programmes' contribution to change, rather than frameworks which focus solely on changes attributable to development programmes – 'that seek to claim the entire credit for change' (Batliwala 2011a, 4).

In their chapter, Carol Miller and Laura Haylock explore the experiences of Oxfam Canada in applying feminist evaluation principles to partnership for monitoring and evaluation. They observe, 'feminist evaluation principles reminded us of whose voices matter most in evaluation and whose stories should count as' (this book, 100). Examples shared come from the Engendering Change women's rights and gender equality programme implemented between 2009 and 2014, with 44 partner organisations in different regions across the world.

MEL, objectivity and feminist insights into 'warring paradigms' of knowledge

In addition to challenging understandings of who is the 'knower', gender-transformative approaches to MEL are using innovative methodologies which challenge reductive understandings of knowledge itself, and the methods by which it is obtained.

In development debates between practitioners and policymakers, considerable time has been spent focusing on the merits of quantitative research methods (that is, research which yields results which are figures-based, countable and therefore often aggregable) versus qualitative methods (yielding data which is not limited to figures and is often descriptive in nature). Of course, real differences between 'quant' and 'qual' are often far less than these stereotypes imply. For example, respondents may be asked to decide whether they agree or disagree with statements numbered along a continuum, and this relies on perceptions rather than any objective reality. In a classic critique, feminist theorist Ann Oakley (2000) highlighted that these debates and frequent disagreements about the validity and status of techniques and types of data masks the real issue, which is a disagreement about 'theories about what knowledge is – ways of framing both knowledge and the means of obtaining it, and how knowers are seen in relation to what is known' (29).

Research approaches based on scientific methods see the purpose of social science research as a way of accessing objectively 'true' facts via structured research, which tests hypotheses to get to the bottom of what works, and what doesn't, in which contexts. It typically involves counting and controlled measurement. Traditionally, this research is seen as value-free, and the relationship of the researcher and 'subject' is understood to be distant and independent. The data which is created is 'hard', reliable, and replicable. Researchers seeking quality aim for things like rigour, reliability, replicability, strength of 'proof', and statistical significance. This vision of research can be summarised as rooted in an idea of objective, scientific knowledge that exists somehow 'outside' the minds of the learner and is available to all to obtain if they follow scientific processes.

This view of researching knowledge contrasts with a very different one, which sees its purpose as discovery, and the generation of knowledge through observing and describing what happens in a 'thick' and highly context-dependent way. It involves observing, focusing on the experience of individual knowers, and often enabling them to describe their particular experience. The data collected are worked out during the study, patterns and events are analysed, and the researcher is often considered an insider, and a participant – very much an actor and influencer of the very system being explored. Many different perceptions, taken together, can provide a rounded picture of what has gone on – but this is an impression that looks different from various angles, rather than an accurate, fixed snapshot of reality.

Coming from this perspective, the idea that one single interpretation of reality can be privileged above all the others, and understood as the sole objective 'truth', suggests that one person's reality trumps the realities of all the others. When funders are footing the bill, MEL practitioners may face intentional or unintentional pressure to privilege one perspective or way of knowing, perpetuating rather than challenging hierarchical social relations. In an applied profession where findings and judgements of value are required, gender-aware MEL practitioners must practise in a way that balances methodological quality, utility and ethics.

In their chapter drawing on the experience of the Swiss bilateral development organisation HELVETAS, Jane Carter and colleagues explore MEL in relation to three projects supported by HELVETAS which focused on different dimensions of empowerment of women. They observe, 'value for money seems to require quantifiable facts. Nevertheless we wonder if better communication on the part of development professionals could mitigate this demand' (this book, 136).

It is growing clearer that mixed methods approaches to research and evaluation can result in strong designs which offers promising ways to approach the complex dilemmas outlined above. The ODI review discussed by Paola Pereznieto and Georgia Taylor in this book, which distilled knowledge about monitoring, evaluation and learning methods and approaches being used in 70 cases, concluded that mixed (quantitative and qualitative) methods are required if economic empowerment is to be evaluated well.

Emily Hillenbrand et al.'s chapter on Helen Keller International's Fish on Farms intervention in Cambodia, mentioned earlier, also provides an excellent example of a project evaluation where the authors have moved beyond simplistic debates about quantitative versus qualitative research methods, aiming to integrate cutting-edge quantitative methods with strong complimentary qualitative inquiry. Fish on Farms aimed also to incorporate the Social Relations Approach as a 'lens' through which to view findings throughout the evaluative system; an ambitious and impressive undertaking.

Increasingly, research and MEL practitioners recognize the value and strength of incorporating a mix of both quantitative and qualitative data and approaches. New research and evaluation methods look to bridge old boundaries – systematically integrating participation into impact evaluation, into statistics, or using a range of data collection and analysis tools and techniques to illuminate very complicated or complex change or to generate and test hypotheses at nearly the same time. These new methods are intentionally sitting qualitative and quantitative data alongside each other, building a jig-saw picture from both kinds of pieces. They use complicated or multi-step methods, employ technology in interesting ways, often involve either mul-timedia or 'big data' or user-generated findings, and adapt well-established methods with variations. An example of the latter is the use of participatory research methods in conjunction with a rigorous approach to sampling – one method of 'participatory statistics' (Holland 2013).

These new ways of exploring both what is 'telling' and what is 'typical' offer welcome news for gender and development specialists acquainted with the work of Ann Oakley and others. It seems we are really progressing towards developing research methodologies that enable us to do this – and do it with, rather than to, research participants.

Responses from development organisations: the art of the possible

All chapters provide case studies of attempts to use mixed methods as well as possible in contexts in which there are resource constraints – particularly on time and money, but also the skills and knowledge of staff in development funding organisations and in the local organisations with whom they work. This is the 'art of the possible' – a challenge that is all-too-familiar to evalua-tors and women's rights activists alike.

Organisation-wide learning systems

A number of chapters focus on creating 'M&E systems' for entire organisations or programmes of work across different contexts, or 'learning systems' for projects. Monitoring and evaluation systems are required which systemati-cally bring different voices and perspectives into sense-making and valuing processes. We understand this to include more than a technical challenge ('how do we store and organize data?'), but one that raises questions of how data is analysed and used, and by whom. Organisations need MEL systems that intentionally identify and involve different stakeholders, including shar-ing of information and analysis with and among them. They also carve out spaces to do intentional reflection and analysis on process and progress, rather than being caught in the busy-ness of 'delivery' – recognising the value of learning generated by programmatic activity.

In their chapter focusing on CARE, Nidal Karim and colleagues share the experience of developing the Women's Empowerment Impact Measurement Initiative (WEIMI) as a response to the organisation's desire to demonstrate impact on gender equality and women's empowerment. WEIMI was imple-mented from 2010 to 2012 in country programmes which had prioritised working with women and/or girls and were designing a programme to last 10–15 years, aiming to achieve – and demonstrate – 'long-term, sustainable change in the lives of women and girls' (this book, p.16). This chapter pro-vides valuable detailed analysis of the process of developing the WEIMI and the analytical tools that which are useful in an impact measurement system. International non governmental organizations (NGO) in particular are interested in such multi-site learning systems, to more widely facilitate improvements in organisational practice.

Obtaining a balance between headline reporting and nuanced findings

Feminists working in MEL often find themselves between a rock and a hard place. Donors want measurable results which offer dramatic, irrefutable evidence of big impact and dramatic change. The truth is so much more than this, and looks different to different people. Progress is sporadic in pace and sometimes apparently discouraging, as one small change leads to backlash and short-term negative impact – battles may be lost and need to be reported on, a long time before the more positive news comes through that the war is about to be won.

Claiming big wins is tempting, if development workers wish to secure the support and funds they need for the work from the powerful. They would like clear demonstrations of results. On the other hand, achieving change of the ambitious kind women require requires long-term work from development organisations, and partnerships with the international women's movements who have long experience of struggles for political and social justice. This work takes place against a backdrop of wider changes which are beyond any organisation – or state – to control. The role of planned development interventions in achieving such vast goals as 'gender equality' in large, complex systems, will often be modest and best understood with the benefit of time.

In MEL, what many powerful stakeholders seek is sharp, clear, definite information which can be assessed, compared, and contrasted. There are deep desires and strong, rational reasons to want to find MEL methods which deliver the clearest information possible on results, and which maybe will also go one step further into giving insights on how to work in the same way in other contexts, to replicate and repeat good results in order to benefit others. Development organisations want to get as clear a picture of the impact of their programming on people as they possibly can; to improve their work in the present and future, to account to funders that their resources have been wisely and effectively used. Donors and large NGOs (or multi-site programmes and projects) often want comparability, which allows them to compare 'investments' across contexts, among other things.

Sometimes MEL staff will have to respond to a demand for comparisons across sites. But pressure to simply compare very different programmes in different contexts is dangerous. As stated earlier, while gender inequality is not the exception but the rule worldwide, the ways in which this plays out are highly context-specific. Similarly, understandings of what constitutes women's empowerment vary from place to place, among individual women and women's groups, and among the staff and consultants employed to evaluate empowerment projects (Kabeer 1998). It is extremely difficult to resolve these issues – sometimes impossible – and efforts to create context-neutral measurement systems can come at the cost of of focus on context-specific factors. Metrics available for use by researchers necessarily usually reveal information that is general, focusing on what we might term 'lowest common denominator' information. For example, commonly-cited international gender-focused metrics include gender-disaggregated literacy rates, the average age of marriage, the average number of children a woman bears. These are obviously critical to know to understand change in a given context, and they can be immensely useful in informing the planning and implementation of many development initiatives. However, we know that such statistics rarely give the whole picture, and more nuanced understanding is required to design appropriate interventions (and MEL plans) for a local context. If women are literate, educated, and having children later, but still not earning the same as men – why is that? Is it an issue of regulation or workplace discrimination? Norms around gendered work? The type of jobs that women take, and the degree of choice they have to decide? All of the above? The answers to important and common questions around women's empowerment are likely to vary – and be illuminated by more granular data – across a range of contexts. There is also a common tension between reporting nuanced, context-specific messaging, and giving a 'big picture' in which results are easily conveyed to non-specialists, and preferably comparable across programmes, and between programmes.

In their chapter focusing on the Women's Empowerment Effectiveness Reviews in Oxfam GB, David Bishop and Kimberly Bowman discuss findings from reviews of projects in more than a dozen sites over three years. Organisational requirements were that MEL specialists evolved 'an approach that could be applied appropriately in a range of contexts, while also producing data that could be aggregated at cross-national or global level, for use by senior managers and for donor reporting' (this book, 255). Aggregating results posed a real challenge in an area of work in which context is so critical.

Working in an empowering way with partner organisations

In her writing on MEL from the perspective of an activist involved in women's rights movement-building for many years, Srilatha Batliwala summarises the need for a new contract between development funders and local women's rights organisations to ensure MEL processes are as empowering as possible for the latter:

> … both donors and women's rights organisations need a paradigm shift in our approach to monitoring and evaluation. Because social power structures and the injustices they create are both resilient and powerful, and it is very difficult indeed to achieve lasting changes in gender relations; because any kind of social change is unpredictable, and the pathways to it are constantly shifting; and above all, because every social change intervention – especially on behalf of women – is an uneven

contrast between meagrely-resourced change activists and powerfully entrenched interests. (Batliwala 2011a, 7)

In her chapter focusing on Womankind Worldwide's experience of MEL in women's rights programmes – in particular focusing on violence against women and girls – Helen Lindley discusses an attempt to develop a monitoring and evaluation system which reflected Womankind's partnership values: to work in coordination with partners, to engage partners in the design of MEL tools and frameworks, and to strengthen not only Womankind's reporting, but partners own monitoring and evaluating systems. This attention to capacity-building is important as rather than assuming partners can and will adopt specific MEL approaches to fit in with donors, this approach potentially enables them to work with other partners, and independently.

In turn, Carol Miller and Laura Haylock's chapter on Oxfam Canada explores tensions between the organisation's stated position in MEL as a 'co-learner' with its partners, and attempts to satisfy donor reporting requirements which 'created an imperative to aggregate results and foster programme learning across the diverse set of partners and largely locally-designed and implemented projects' (this book, 293).

The technical is political! Using MEL to dispel myths and change policies and practices

It is essential for gender and MEL specialists to take the best offered by feminist theories and existing approaches to MEL, but to remain open to learning and evolving new ways of assessing the impact of development on women and men, women's rights, and gender equality. There is a considerable risk that, should we not take up this challenge, such MEL will continue to be done to women, rather than with and for them. Remarkable advancements in social science and information technology hold great promise for helping us to understand the nature of complex and adaptive social change. Should we choose not to understand and master these new tools, we risk applying them incorrectly, or worse, seeing issues of power and complexity pushed aside in favour of technocratic simplicity and 'quick fixes'. It is our ethical and human responsibility to understand how systematic inquiry can be put to use for poor women and men.

In their chapter focusing on the work of the International Rescue Committee in the Democratic Republic of Congo (DRC), Marie-France Guimond and Katie Robinette focus on to how results gained from MEL can be used to improve the work of development organisations responding to the needs of women, girls, men and boys at grassroots level, and in advocacy and campaigning to inform government and international policy priorities. They discuss how myths about violence against women and girls (VAWG) can be 'busted' using programme data. The IRC collects data routinely as part of its support to survivors of VAWG. The data provides a valuable resource for future programme and policy planning – forming the all-important baseline data which some other authors in this issue highlight as missing when MEL begins.

Conclusion

Despite its immense importance, MEL is all-too-often viewed reductively as a technical realm, rather than the political one that it really is. It may be dismissed as consisting of repetitious, time-consuming technical tasks, involving flow charts, logical frameworks and lists of 'indicators' which need to be generated in order to keep donors and managers happy and 'feed the beast'. When we considered how we wanted to commission this book, a very important factor was the need to challenge this reductive view of an essential part of development and humanitarian work.

We hope that we have succeeded to some extent in doing this through featuring some really interesting and inspiring case studies of different approaches to MEL. These attempt to tell the story of change through a gendered lens, through systematised information and management systems that honour the experiences and power of partner organisations, and individual women and men. Part of the process of transforming development policies and programmes to meet the interests and satisfy the needs of women and girls involves transforming the way we learn, monitor and evaluate how and if our efforts affect changes in attitudes, gender roles, and power relations between the sexes. We are, hence, required to learn about changes relating to our activities through the eyes of all individuals and groups affected by planned development and humanitarian work, and to consider the issue of power and inequality in relation to MEL itself.

References

Batliwala, Srilatha (2011a) *Strengthening Monitoring and Evaluation for Women's Rights: Thirteen Insights for Women's Organizations* (2011a), Toronto: AWID, www.awid.org/Library/Strengthening-Monitoring-and-Evaluation-for-Women-s-Rights-Thirteen-Insights-for-Women-s-Organizations (last checked by the authors June 2014)

Batliwala, Srilatha (2011b) *Strengthening Monitoring and Evaluation for Women's Rights: Twelve Insights For Donors*, Toronto, Mexico City, Cape Town: AWID, https://www.awid.org/publications/strengthening-monitoring-and-evaluation-womens-rights-12-insights-donors (last checked by the authors June 2017)

Boserup, Esther (1971) (reprinted 1997 & 2013), *Women's Role in Economic Development*, London: Earthscan

Brisolara, Sharon, Denise Seigart, and Saumitra SenGupta (2014) *Feminist Evaluation and Research: Theory and Practice*, New York and London: The Guildford Press

Chant, Sylvia, and Caroline Sweetman (2012) 'Fixing women or fixing the world? 'Smart economics', efficiency approaches, and gender equality in development', Gender & Development 20(3): 517–529

Elson, Diane (1995) Male Bias in the Development Process, Manchester: Manchester University Press

Holland, J (2013), *Who Counts? The Power of Participatory Statistics*. Institute of Development Studies (IDS): Brighton. Available at http://www.ids.ac.uk/publication/who-counts-the-power-of-participatory-statistics (checked by authors 2 July 2017).

Kabeer, Naila (1994) *Reversed Realities: Gender Hierarchies In Development Thought*, London and New York: Verso

Kabeer, Naila (1998) *Money Can't Buy Me Love? Re-evaluating Gender, Credit and Empowerment in Rural Bangladesh*, IDS Discussion Paper 363, Brighton: Institute of Development Studies

O'Donnell, Amy, (2015), 'A rights-based approach to responsible data', blog-post available at http://policy-practice.oxfam.org.uk/blog/2015/08/a-rights-based-approach-to-treating-data-responsibly (last checked by the authors June 2017)

March, Candida, Ines Smyth and Maitrayee Mukhopadhyay (1999) *A Guide to Gender-Analysis Frameworks*, Oxford: Oxfam GB

Moser, Caroline (1993) *Gender Planning and Development*, London: Routledge

Oakley, Ann (2000) *Experiments in Knowing: gender and method in the social sciences*, Cambridge: Polity Press

Sen, Gita, and Caren Grown (1987) *Development Crises and Alternative Visions: Third World Women's Perspectives*, DAWN, New York: Monthly Review Press (available as a pdf at: http://www.dawnnet.org/feminist-resources/sites/default/files/articles/devt_crisesalt_visions_sen_and_grown.pdf (last checked by the authors June 2017)

Young, Kate, Carol Wolkowitz and Roslyn McCullagh (eds.) (1981) *Of Marriage and the Market: Women's Subordination Internationally and its Lessons*, London: Routledge & Kegan Paul

About the authors

Kimberly Bowman is the Programme Quality Team Manager in Oxfam GB's Programme Strategy and Impact team. Postal address, Oxfam House, John Smith Drive, Oxford OX4 2JY, UK. Email: kbowman@oxfam.org.uk

Caroline Sweetman is Editor of Gender & Development. Postal address: Oxfam House, John Smith Drive, Oxford OX4 2JY, UK. Email: csweetman@oxfam.org.uk

CHAPTER 2

Building capacity to measure long-term impact on women's empowerment: CARE's Women's Empowerment Impact Measurement Initiative

Nidal Karim, Mary Picard, Sarah Gillingham and Leah Berkowitz

Abstract

From 2010 to 2012, CARE USA implemented the Women's Empowerment Impact Measurement Initiative (WEIMI) to develop the necessary capacity, tools, guidance, and practice to measure and demonstrate the impact of its work on women's empowerment. The lessons and experiences from this initiative have been transformed into an online guidance tool being utilised throughout CARE to inform the process of developing robust theories of change and impact measurement systems for women's empowerment programmes. The WEIMI experience has contributed significantly to CARE's understanding of gender inequality and its implications for achieving broader impact. This chapter highlights key lessons learned and good practices that emerged in addressing the challenge of developing organisational impact measurement systems for women's empowerment long-term programmes.

Keywords: gender, theory of change, impact measurement, impact groups, social change

Background

CARE,[1] with its organisational commitment to women's empowerment and gender equality, has engaged in various efforts around the measurement of women's empowerment and gender equality. In 2010, CARE USA launched the Women's Empowerment Impact Measurement Initiative (WEIMI) as a way to respond to one of the organisation's key strategic priorities to demonstrate impact. This priority evolved from two critical processes that CARE had engaged in – a Strategic Impact Inquiry (SII) on women's empowerment; and a re-orientation in its programming to long-term programmes (LTPs) as the core of its country office development strategy.[2] The SII was a multi-year,

http://dx.doi.org/10.3362/9781780447049.002

multi-country study from 2004 to 2009 whose results showed that CARE as an organisation needed to improve its capacity to demonstrate long-term, sustainable change in the lives of women and girls.[3] In the latter instance, the shift to LTPs set in motion a process of organisational change to absorb projects or short-term initiatives into a coherent programme of 10–15 years whose goal aligned with a specific impact group. While country offices were not required to focus on women and girls, their own inquiries, in the process of developing new programmes, led most of them to prioritise women and/or girls as their 'impact groups' – that is, social groups whose lives they wished to change.

WEIMI was implemented from 2010 to 2012 with a small set of country offices which had prioritised women and/or girls for one or more of their LTPs and were still in the design stage, developing a theory of change (TOC) as the basis for planning, implementing, monitoring, and evaluation. WEIMI's focus was to build capacity to measure change; however, the initiative also aimed to highlight the strategies that could be used in a successful empowerment approach, as well as deepen the experience in gender transformative programming to addressing poverty. In the process of engaging with country teams, it became apparent that working with key women's empowerment and gender-sensitive indicators in the country context of LTPs required assistance to country teams so they could develop coherent and robust theories of change. Lessons about best practice were harvested from the experiences of this group of country offices and used to create guidance for other country offices. The online guidance tool developed from this process is available at http://gendertoolkit.care.org/weimi/introduction.aspx (last checked by the authors January 2014).

In the larger context of the international development field, what CARE attempted through WEIMI was ground-breaking and innovative, and generated considerable learning. In this chapter, we will present some of the good practices and lessons learned in proceeding from the phase of conceptualising theories of change to a new phase of developing the basic elements of an impact measurement system for LTPs, focused on women's empowerment and gender equality.

First, though, we offer some definitions of terms which we used throughout this work, and discuss in this paper.

Good practices

The country offices which participated in WEIMI were at different stages of developing their LTPs at the time this initiative got under way. The documentation and sharing of experiences within and between technical staff in country offices and headquarters, and consultants providing support to country offices, gave shape to the guidance document which consolidated three principal stages of measuring impact – developing the TOC, developing the impact measurement system, and testing the TOC.

Development of the TOC

In the process of conceptualising LTPs, country office teams had only recently been introduced to the concepts defined in Table 2.1, such as *domains of change, pathways of change, breakthroughs,* and *strategic hypotheses* as components of a TOC. Because these concepts were unfamiliar, this stage of the

Table 2.1 Definitions

Theory of change	Generically, a set of hypotheses (if–then statements) and critical assumptions and risks underpinning the design for how the programme goal will be achieved. In the context of a programme, this generic definition is represented by the pathways of change which flow from domains of change and are marked by breakthroughs.[a]
Domains of change	Areas in which change is essential to achieving an impact goal. A goal may have a corresponding set of two to four domains of change. Domains of change can be seen as critical preconditions, or major outcomes, required to be in place for the impact goal to be achieved.[a]
Pathways of change	The conditions necessary for achieving a domain of change(s) and the assumptions that support these conditions. Together, they 'tell the story' of how you expect the change to happen. These assumptions are the causal links between conditions.[b]
Breakthroughs	A change that represents a significant leap forward that is not easily reversed. It represents a change that affects both the breadth of impact (increasing impact on many more people in our impact group) and the depth of impact (increasing the level of well-being or transformation in the lives of our impact group). The change resulting from a breakthrough is reflected in the lives of people in the impact group, as well as people in the impact group outside the programme's operational areas.[a]
Strategic hypotheses	Hypotheses that are vital to the success of achieving the programme goal and for which no empirical evidence exists to date. Their results will inform the programme strategy and possibly result in a refinement of the theory of change.[c]
Impact group	The specific population group upon which the programme (CARE and its partners) aims to have a positive impact with a long-term commitment to overcome their underlying causes of poverty and social injustice. The scale of the impact on this group is at least at the national level.[a]
Sub-impact group	One of the disaggregated groups that share the characteristics of the impact group but also has other unique characteristics that differ from those of the impact group as a whole. Specific programme initiatives that form part of an overarching programme may need to focus on a subset population.[a]
Target group	Those who will be consistently targeted and will require a target strategy for behaviour change. This can be done either through direct investment or an influencing strategy.[a] Typically, target groups for women's empowerment programmes will include men and boys, religious leaders, civil society actors, political leaders, and government organisations, all of which have to be empirically defined.

(Continue)

Table 2.1 Definitions (*Continued*)

Stakeholder group	Those who may affect or be affected by the programme and are recognised for their importance in co-operating or collaborating with the programme; but they are not necessarily targeted by the programme activities.[a]

[a] *During the shift to a programme approach in CARE, a set of guidance notes was developed to facilitate the change process across CARE.* Brief No. 5: Designing Programmes *was on designing long-term programmes and included some basic definitions to accompany the p-shift process, such as theory of change, domain of change, and breakthrough. The brief can be found at:* http://p-shift.care2share.wikispaces.net/file/view/Brief%236_Designing%20programs_14%20Sept2009.pdf *(last checked 14 January 2014). The definition provided in the brief for 'theory of change' matches with the original conceptualisation presented by Carol Weiss (1995) and how it was further elaborated by Anderson (2004). The terms 'domains of change' and 'breakthroughs' as defined in the brief, were coined by the authors of the brief (Michael Drinkwater and Mary Picard).*
[b] *The term 'pathway of change' was used somewhat loosely during the programme shift and this definition was proposed during the WEIMI support process as a working definition by Mary Picard. For more details, see the WEIMI guidance tool at:* http://gendertoolkit.care.org/weimi/introduction.aspx *(last checked 14 January 2014).*
[c] *The term 'strategic hypothesis' came about during the WEIMI support process, in the work with CARE Tanzania, to aid the country office in moving from the conceptual to the practical: that is, to prioritise the critical hypothesis to be tested in the immediate term.*

process involved a larger-than-expected share of the time and resources the WEIMI technical team had allocated for capacity-building. However, this substantial investment of time and resources generated considerable lessons for CARE on the process of developing robust theories of change for women's empowerment programmes pursuing long-term, sustainable change.

From the WEIMI experience, several critical features of a good TOC for women's empowerment emerged:

- The conceptualising of the TOC must be led by the ultimate aim of gender equality and must not narrowly conceive working exclusively with women and girls as the path because structural and social changes necessary for gender equality requires that everyone in society, including men and boys, change their behaviours and attitudes.
- Based on the premise that achieving gender equality is not a zero-sum game, it is essential to contextualise empowerment of women and girls through sound analysis that incorporates and elevates the perspectives of women and girls, without ignoring those of men and boys.[4]
- It is also critically important to include stakeholders from a broad spectrum in the discussion of the TOC and its validation. In the case of women and girls belonging to the impact group, it is best to solicit their input as source material for the TOC, as most country offices did.
- Both short-term and long-term change occurs as a result of any planned development intervention, and this should be kept in mind. This means short-term results in particular should be seen in perspective. Some gains will be achieved more quickly, while others, such as changes in harmful social norms, will take longer and will require an investment in

relationships with those who share the vision of the TOC and can help bring about broader and longer-term change.

- There is an imperative to go beyond project or programme-level goals to achieve gender-equitable behaviours among individuals to programming that aims at larger gender-equitable social norms, systems, policies, and structures.

In addition, some *key good practices* emerged from the country office experiences on how to ensure the quality and robustness of TOCs for women's empowerment programmes.

1. Carry out a *vulnerability analysis*, which includes a gender as part of analysis.

This involves examining the causes of vulnerability specific to women and girls (and as distinct from men and boys) in a country-specific context. *All* women have vulnerabilities, that are specific to phases of the life cycle (prenatal–infancy–childhood–adolescence–adulthood), such as those associated with sexual and reproductive health problems or with gender-based violence. Additionally, dimensions such as wealth category, socio-cultural context, livelihood security, and ethnic or religious affiliation overlap with the life-cycle dimension to explain vulnerabilities that affect women differently *over their whole life cycle*. This kind of vulnerability analysis includes an articulation of the physical, social, economic, and psychological manifestations of vulnerability for women and girls.

Example: CARE Bangladesh did a Causes and Consequences tree exercise as part of a vulnerability analysis. The team first identified the underlying causes of vulnerability for women and girls as distinct from those of men and boys. They then articulated the physical, psychological, social, economic, and political manifestations of vulnerability, marginalisation, or exploitation. And as a third step, they identified the groups of women and girls for whom the vulnerabilities applied.[5] Based on the findings of their analysis, they were then able to generate an understanding of degrees of marginalisation of women (see Figure 2.1).

2. Have clear definitions of *impact* and *sub-impact groups*.

This is important because they determine what changes amongst whom must be measured, i.e. the unit of analysis and sampling frame (see Table 2.1 for definitions).

Clear identification of sub-impact groups helps build an advocacy agenda around a social justice issue pertaining to a specific population group. The findings of the vulnerability analysis provide guidance for drawing boundaries around the impact group and then prioritising which population groups to select as *sub-impact groups*. Grounding impact group definitions in analysis in this way is a core good practice. Those country offices that began this way found that their process was smoother, because it anchored decision-making

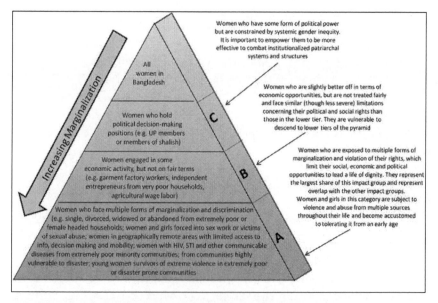

Figure 2.1 CARE Bangladesh: 'women' differentiated by degree of marginalisation

in a transparent process, so that over time, questions about the impact group (its characteristics and delineation) would always revert back to the analysis and not be susceptible to individual perspectives of who the impact group is or should be.

Example: Figure 2.2 illustrates CARE Burundi's analysis of impact and sub-impact groups. The latter are not always discrete sub-population groups. Yet, one proceeds from analysis to a decision on the strategy to address the needs of sub-impact groups or to prioritise them for programming.

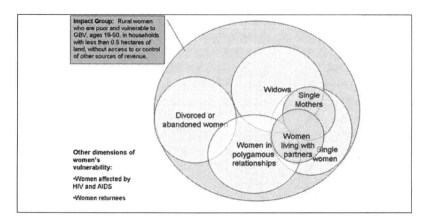

Figure 2.2 CARE Burundi's analysis of impact and sub-impact groups

3. Engage in a systematic process to identify *target groups* and *stakeholder groups* (see Table 2.1 for definitions).

Knowledge about the behaviours and positioning of both is important for deciding which groups to target or influence and with which groups a programme should be developing strategic relations. Most of the WEIMI country offices identified broad target groups as a starting point, such as men and boys, religious leaders, political leaders, civil society actors, and government organisations. However, they then had to go beyond general categories to empirical specificity – which civil society organisations, which men, which community leaders, and so on. While CARE has often worked in alliance with different stakeholders and target groups, the LTPs pushed country offices to understand more deeply how different target groups and stakeholders contribute to impact goals and how to work collaboratively towards these shared goals, with a focus on strategic – rather than instrumental – engagement.

Example: CARE Tanzania carried out a stakeholder analysis for their Women's Empowerment Long Term Programme as part of a partnership strategy. The resulting document lists organisations key to the achievement of

---

Tanzania Stakeholder Analysis and Mapping

The Tanzania Stakeholder Analysis and Mapping categorised stakeholders as follows:
I.   Government organisations
II. Other institutions / structures
   • CBOs/Traditional Structures (Formal and Informal), Interest Groups, Religious Institutions/ Organisations, etc
   • Social movements
   • Local NGOs
   • International NGOs
   • Research institutions
   • UN agencies and multilaterals
   • Other funders/ donors
   • Others [Bilateral Organisations, Individuals (Role Models, Positive Deviants), Negative Contributors (Brokers, Circumcisers, Traditional Leaders), etc.

It then mapped stakeholders according to level of engagement with impact groups with these column headings:
   • Organisation
   • Degree of overlap with impact groups
   • Specific focus on sub-impact group
   • The kind of relationship expected with the programme (stakeholder group, target group, or impact group)
   • Degree of similarity of vision and mission
   • Current and potential influence and contribution to scale
   • Degree of interest in partnership and the TOC
   • Type of relationship expected in the context of the TOC (with choice of policy partner, Implementation, Research, Co-funding, Other)
   • Kind of financing relationship expected

Its recommendations proposed partnerships using this categorisation:
   • Strategic
   • Intermediary
   • Implementing
   • Informal (non-monetary)

Figure 2.3 Tanzania stakeholder analysis and mapping

breakthrough points, major risks/threats of each organisation to the TOC, and proposed mitigation measures. Figure 2.3 illustrates the steps included in their stakeholder analysis.

4. Invite diverse stakeholders to review the team's holistic analysis and to solicit their expert advice.

This can be done periodically, from the first draft of a problem tree or a vulnerability analysis underlying the selection of impact groups, and at other points during the development of the TOC and the measurement tools.

For example, in the case of the development of the TOC for CARE Egypt's programme, the team clarified the value of diverse perspectives. They systematically gathered input from their impact group to inform the TOC exercise. Women's organisations and activists provided a legal and rights approach; United Nations (UN) agencies offered an institutional and policy perspective; peer international non-government organisations (NGOs) contributed to the quality and thoroughness of the approach and presented possibilities for strategic partnerships in areas of common interest; and donors and community-based organisations ensured relevance of the TOC to the lives of women in local communities. Inviting the perspective of a relevant ministry (e.g. the Ministry of Women and Children) was also important to ensure harmonisation with a government plan or strategy for gender and development.

5. Think strategically and proactively about relationship building with other civil society actors, groups, and other fora at different levels.

This will encourage social activism and an emergent social movement advocating for equal rights fulfilment. Critical reflection is needed on the supportive role a programme plays to build the confidence of impact group members and their allies to lead, and to advocate for, the changes they desire in their lives. Challenging unequal gender power relations means confronting rights abuses and forms of discrimination. The programme's role as a powerbroker and in stimulating, facilitating, or supporting a social movement depends considerably on how it manages its relations with others.

For example, CARE Egypt was aware of its positioning amongst civil society actors, which offered it an opportunity to promote women's rights. The country team invited activists, practitioners, UN agencies and other players to validate its TOC, and foster links to enable it to collaborate routinely with other actors on all initiatives. One of CARE's tactics was to build on its membership in the Network of Women's Rights Organisations with the German governmental aid agency GTZ (Deutsche Gesellschaft für Internationale Zusammenarbeit or the German Organisation for Technical Cooperation). This made it possible for CARE to participate in presenting a Shadow Report to the UN Committee, and, with the National Council for Women, to be part of a broader coalition monitoring the Egyptian government's performance against CEDAW (the 1979 international Convention on the Elimination of

Discrimination Against Women) that addresses women's economic and social rights. Prior to submitting the Shadow Report, CARE conducted awareness training with 30 civil society organisations, including media and religious leaders, in relation to CEDAW. This concluded in their making a commitment to work on promoting women's rights with a focus on the anti-gender-based violence law and Personal Status Law.[6]

According to the CARE Egypt team, the networking and joint planning efforts enabled community organisations to build and develop their networks of community members, increasing their reach. CARE found that the village savings and loans associations (VSLAs) provided a vehicle at grassroots level for women's voices. Other organisations such as Plan Egypt, an international NGO working to fulfil the rights of children, began building on joint work to amend the Personal Status Law and make other policy changes. CARE Egypt's LTP continues to identify a more comprehensive set of actors with whom to collaborate in the future to achieve broader changes for women and girls.

6. Recognise that social change is not linear and not all conditions that account for change can be predicted.

Formulating a TOC is about making explicit assumptions about the social change process over a projected period of time. As new evidence arises while a development programme runs, the TOC can be re-validated and refined. Country offices constructing a TOC found that a key step was to develop the expected outcomes contributing to their programmes' impact goals, i.e. the *domains of change* (DOCs).

Example: Figure 2.4 shows part of the TOC from CARE Bangladesh for their Women's Empowerment LTP and illustrates how they created DOCs linked to their impact goal.

7. Make sure pathways of change, which are cause–effect assumptions that represent the critical hypotheses for achieving one or more DOCs, are accompanied by a clear justification and explanation, reflecting the team's current state of knowledge.

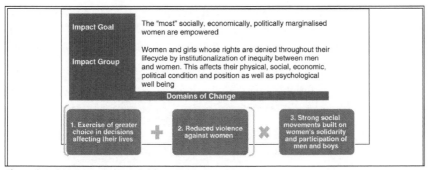

Figure 2.4 CARE Bangladesh DOCs and impact goal

They must also be specific about *whose* behaviours or roles need to change in order to attain the highest level result of a pathway. Based on the WEIMI experiences, the number of pathways should not exceed 12, across three to four DOCs.

Developing an impact measurement system

The next stage of the process – developing the impact measurement system – was initiated once the TOC for the women's empowerment LTP was complete, recognising that *pathways of change* would continue to be refined and substantiated. Elements of the impact measurement system at this stage consisted of indicators at several levels, *strategic hypotheses, breakthroughs*, and monitoring of trends, risks, and assumptions.

A few of the good practices from this stage that have wider relevance are:

1. Ensure a comprehensive definition of 'impact' in the context of women's empowerment.

The WEIMI country offices used CARE's definition of women's empowerment which is based on CARE's SII research and the broader literature, as well as work that CARE Norway undertook to consider women's empowerment indicators beyond those identified through the Millennium Development Goals and Indicators (MDGs/MDIs). The definition conceptualises women's empowerment as the sum total of the changes needed for a woman to realise her full human rights with the changes being an interplay of her own aspirations and capabilities (agency), the power relations through which she must navigate (relations), and the environment that surrounds and conditions her choices (structure).[7] In the context of this definition, 'impact' as such is the attainment of rights, occurring over a longer-term time horizon, to reflect the slow pace of much social change. This means that if gains made by women and girls under a programme are incremental (e.g. improvements in rates of girls' retention in school) but not sustained by deeper social change that is grounded in changing power relations, then the programme impact goals of rights attainment will be elusive.

An example is CARE Burundi's impact goal: by 2025, poor women, aged from 18 to 50, vulnerable to gender-based violence, from rural households with less than 0.5 hectares of land property, without access or control over other sources of income, have regained their dignity and fully enjoy their basic rights.

2. Develop a diverse set of indicators that are reflective of the multidimensionality of women's empowerment and is responsive to the local context. Country teams were encouraged (but not required) to choose from a proposed standard menu of the MDI indicators, each with a grouping of outcome-level indicators (corresponding to the domain of change level). Across the WEIMI countries, the most frequently used indicators were:

    *   percentage of men and women reporting meaningful participation of women in the public sphere;

- percentage of men and women with changed attitudes towards gender-based violence;
- percentage of households with access to secure land tenure, by sex of the head of household;
- percentage of men and women reporting ability of women to control productive assets effectively;
- percentage of women reporting meaningful participation in decision-making at household level in a domain previously reserved for men;
- percentage of households with capacity to cope with environmental shocks without depleting assets, by sex of the head of household.

The span of the six indicators reflects and affirms the multi-dimensional nature of women's empowerment. Most of these indicators refer to issues which are fundamental to changes in conditions across the domains of CARE's women's empowerment framework – agency, relations, and structure.[8] However, while some success was attained in standardising measures of women's empowerment, the experience of the WEIMI country offices as they put these indicators into use showed that they had to be further adapted to the contexts and specific population groups.

3. Expect the design of indicators and hypotheses to be iterative, resulting in a final round of refinement of the TOC so that it is specific enough for measurement purposes.
   Typically, this process produces more 'sense-making' in the group until agreement is reached on the most feasible and priority indicators and hypotheses.

4. Guide the process of developing elements of the measurement system with a set of filter questions that remind the team of important principles and good measurement practice.

Examples of the filter questions CARE used are listed below; some will need to be adapted for other organisations. It is good to pause and reflect on these from time to time.

- Gender disaggregation: are you designing your measurement systems with the capacity to disaggregate all data by sex (comparing males to females)?
- CARE's empowerment framework: do the measurement elements altogether capture changes across multiple levels? The WEIMI country offices utilised the categories of agency, structure, and relations from CARE's empowerment framework and it has been especially important to measure change in structure and relations (i.e. not to privilege agency above the other two).
- Inclusion of men and boys: are you including men and boys in measurement of behaviour change at the target group level?
- Impact: are you capturing both breadth (scale) and depth of impact?

- Unexpected outcomes: are there any expected changes in the overall TOC that are not being captured and may actually be slipping through the measurement cracks?
5. Make sure to identify and measure pathway indicators in addition to impact and outcome indicators.

This ensures that the impact measurement system is able to document not only whether there are changes but also 'how' the changes are happening. A practice that most WEIMI country offices found useful was to map individual projects to pathways at an early stage, before finalising the measurement system. Making the link between the conceptual and the 'real world' provides an opportunity for teams to bring their programmatic knowledge to bear on formulating pathway indicators. This process also provides a mechanism to map projects from multiple sectors on to particular women's empowerment-focused outcome and impact goals.

Progress after WEIMI

Although WEIMI came to an end as a specific initiative in 2012, the fruits of CARE's investment did not end then. Most of the WEIMI country offices continued to make progress on their own and many other country offices have used the guidance developed under WEIMI to inform their processes of developing impact measurement systems for women's empowerment programmes. Experiences of progress to date by some of the country offices (both WEIMI and non-WEIMI) that were reported at a convening in late 2013 are shared below.

CARE Bangladesh staff highlighted several current core practices that have emerged as a result of their WEIMI engagement. These included:

- the ongoing consistent use of tools and techniques developed from WEIMI;
- observance of a standard evaluation policy and research framework;
- establishment of linkages for sharing and drawing learning within and beyond the CARE world across a range of topics such as women's empowerment, climate change, food security, governance, and engaging men and boys, amongst others;
- development of wide-reaching partnerships with both national (e.g. the International Centre for Diarrhoeal Disease Research, Bangladesh) and international research and academic institutions;
- the establishment of a monitoring and evaluation working group, consisting of staff from multiple levels and programmatic areas, that comes together to share learning and decide on areas that need to be explored in terms of testing hypotheses or carrying out analyses.

CARE Tanzania is strengthening its country office data inflow subsystem specifically around LTP indicators, focusing on data collection and management processes. Staff in Tanzania are also focusing more on 'impact monitoring'

– tracking the contribution of CARE projects towards processes of social change, rather than being focused on indicator data alone.

CARE West Bank Gaza, a non-WEIMI country, used the WEIMI guidance for ideas on indicators and tools for its Gender and Empowerment LTP, and reported that the country office was accordingly able to benefit from the embedded lessons learned and the tools and examples identified there. Staff reported addressing a few of the lessons learned from WEIMI in the following ways:

- developing their impact measurement system at the country office level rather than at the LTP level;
- developing areas of inquiry that span across their LTPs and monitoring indicators within each area (e.g. to what extent are advocacy activities influencing policies, promoting change in social norms, and increasing democratic space?);
- incorporating forward accountability mechanisms into their measurement system.

CARE Uganda has also drawn on the WEIMI guidance to map all of its existing projects into one of four LTPs, which required refocusing the goals of some of the projects. They also consistently use the TOCs for their LTPs as a frame of reference for all new funding opportunities, so that new projects are in alignment with their LTPs and can provide opportunities to test potential pathways to empowerment and hypotheses about it in their TOCs. As the country office has progressed in the development of its LTPs, staff there are continuing to readjust and pilot new forms of relationships with partners, and systems of accountability to partners and community members, as well as working to ensure that staff provide cross-functional support to projects within their LTPs for women's empowerment (as opposed to project-only functions), and convening quarterly programme quality and learning meetings to ensure continuing organisational learning.

Key lessons learned

WEIMI was a ground-breaking and innovative initiative for CARE, which highlighted a number of challenges and resulted in the identification of some critical lessons regarding the development and operationalisation of impact measurement systems to capture the long-term, sustainable, and transformative changes in women's lives. Key lessons learned from the WEIMI experience are outlined below.

Timelines for transformative organisational change

Although WEIMI was originally intended to take country offices through the full process of development of TOCs and measurement systems to testing different parts of the TOCs, the two-year timeline of the initiative was too short. WEIMI was happening on the heels of the shift to a long-term 'programme' approach in CARE, which entailed significant changes in organisational thinking and work routines.[9] At the start of WEIMI, the country offices involved were at different stages of development of their TOCs. The offices needed to manage the work of their on-going project activities at the same time as stepping back to undertake the broader gender, vulnerability, and stakeholder mapping analyses required for the development of their TOCs. At the same time, they needed to build new and different relationships with stakeholders. These multiple requirements proved very demanding. As a result, the WEIMI country offices found it a challenge to get to the point of testing their TOCs over the timeframe of the initiative. One of the critical lessons that emerged from this experience is the need to dedicate human resources to the task of completing the TOC and developing the measurement system, ideally as part of a country office annual operational plan with distributed responsibility.

Linking project-level monitoring and evaluation to long-term programme impact measurement systems

The experience of WEIMI also highlighted the need for country offices to link the impact measurement work with existing projects and programming initiatives so that responsibility for delivery of the TOC outcomes became owned and driven by those project initiatives. While some of the WEIMI country offices mapped their projects on to the long-term programme's TOC, the teams struggled more with the practical process of linking individual project monitoring and evaluation systems to the programme measurement system. This was a reflection of individual projects having their own dedicated monitoring and evaluation databases, systems, and indicators. The technical practicalities of creating the knowledge management infrastructure to link data across multiple projects needed to be consciously prioritised and addressed as early as possible by developing a higher (that is, programme-level) impact measurement system.

Where the 'perfect' becomes the enemy

As WEIMI was essentially breaking new ground and seeking to learn from the group of country offices involved, there was no prescribed path to be followed for the development of their impact measurement systems for their women's empowerment programmes. This created situations in which some country offices got stuck in the first stage of the process, wanting to create a 'perfect' TOC, before moving on to create the infrastructure for their measurement systems and start finding opportunities to collect data.

   A critical lesson learned from the experiences of these country offices was the need to enable programme staff to not let the 'perfect' be the enemy of the 'practical', and to see the different phases of the process as parallel and iterative, rather than linear.

Conclusions

For CARE, WEIMI has embodied a significant learning opportunity on women's empowerment, gender equality, vulnerability, and impact measurement. While the short length of the initiative posed a major challenge, it was able to set the wheels in motion for changes well beyond its duration and to generate learning grounded in the experiences of country office teams that has benefited many who were not directly involved.

Through WEIMI, country office teams were able to explore the complexity of TOCs focused on women's empowerment, and deepen their understanding on how to programme towards the long-term impact goal of gender equality. Country offices were also pushed to expand their understanding of impact groups and have a much more nuanced appreciation of the different levels of marginalisation faced by different groups of women. Altogether, this has contributed to country offices being able to think strategically about, design, and link new projects across different sectors, to contribute to gender-equality goals.

Additionally, amidst the complexity that the process and concept of women's empowerment embodies, CARE was better able to recognise that the long-term goal of gender equality can only be achieved through collective efforts to support gender justice and change for women, across diverse sectors and stakeholders. Hence, the significant emphasis placed through WEIMI on building new relationships, and engaging more diverse stakeholders, helped country offices expand who they partner with and how they partner.

As the broader development field continues to make progress in integrating gender issues into its understandings and analyses of the causes and solutions to poverty and marginalisation, the lessons which come out of initiatives like WEIMI provide critical insights into how to think about women's empowerment and gender equality as overarching goals for all our work. The learning from WEIMI also underlines that we need more initiatives to build the capacity of development policymakers and practitioners to monitor progress, at the same time as generating learning on how to hasten this progress.

Notes

1. Cooperative for Assistance and Relief Everywhere (CARE) was founded in 1945, and is a leading humanitarian organisation fighting global poverty. In the fiscal year 2013, CARE worked in 86 countries, supporting 927 poverty-fighting development and humanitarian aid projects to reach more than 97 million people. CARE USA is a national member of CARE International, a global confederation of 13 National Members and one Affiliate Member with the common goal of fighting global poverty. Each CARE Member is an autonomous NGO and implements programme, advocacy, fundraising, and communications activities in its own country and in developing countries where CARE has programmes. For more information on CARE USA, see www.CARE.org, and for more information on CARE International, see www.care-international.org.

2. LTPs are made up of a coherent set of initiatives that include externally funded projects. Each programme has a focused and long-term commitment (10–15 years) to a specific marginalised and vulnerable group to achieve lasting impact at a broad scale for the designated impact group through addressing underlying causes of poverty and social injustice. This was a key shift in CARE's programmatic approach, that traditionally began with a three to five-year project designed with a sectoral lens to a *programme approach* that began with a holistic analysis of the underlying causes of poverty, marginalisation, and social injustice affecting the lives of a chosen impact group. For more information on CARE's conceptualisation of LTPs, see *Brief No.1: What is a Program Approach* which can be found at: http://p-shift.care2share.wikispaces.net/file/view/Brief%20 No.1_What%20is%20a%20program%20approach.pdf (last checked by the authors April 2014).
3. A multi-year study across 400 projects and 24 countries and drew key insights about women's empowerment work. What was really 'key' about the process was that over 350 staff from around the globe participated and this participatory approach was instrumental to transforming our work globally with a stronger and more robust approach to women's empowerment. Details of the study can be found at: http://pqdl.care.org/sii/ default.aspx (last checked by the authors January 2014).
4. We recognise that alternative conceptualisations of gender equality as a zero-sum game or as a process with benefits for both sexes are a source of much debate in development practice. CARE's stand on this issue is that gender equality will be of collective benefit for all. Instead of viewing men and women as oppositional groups with power transferred from one to the other, CARE recognises the importance of creating new structures and changing attitudes that foster interdependent, mutually supportive relationships, within the context of household, community, and society as a whole. In many contexts this involves challenging and changing existing power relations, challenging how gender roles are shaped and practised for all genders, and recognising that men and boys can also lose out from oppressive gender stereotypes; for example, if aspects of their own identity run counter to hegemonic concepts of masculinity, and when they wish to take on new roles and ways of being in support of gender equality. We recognise that social rules and configurations of masculinity often trap men within a rigid set of what is considered socially acceptable behaviour that may be harmful to themselves and others. Engaging men and boys in gender-equality programming ensures that everyone is making necessary changes and is involved in the process of creating new, more equitably beneficial social structures. The experiences of the CARE country offices participating in WEIMI consistently highlighted the dangers of ignoring the attitudes, behaviours, and needs of men and boys in programming to address gender issues, and the importance of promoting positive masculinity as a mechanism for working to promote gender equality. For a detailed explanation on CARE's focus on gender equality see the *Explanatory Note on CARE's Gender Focus* at: www.careacademy.org/ cheops/Documents/22.%20Explanatory%20Note%20on%20CAREs%20 Gender%20Focus.pdf (last checked by the authors April 2014).

5. The details of this exercise can be found on CARE's Gender Toolkit at: http://gendertoolkit.care.org/pages/Mapping%20Drivers%20of%20 Poverty.aspx (last checked by the authors April 2014).

6. The Personal Status Law in Egypt, Law no. 25, has undergone several amendments since its first codification in 1920. The law regulates matters of marriage, divorce, and child custody, and is governed by Islamic law or Sharia. In the post-revolution period, women's rights activists have been concerned about threats to repeal reforms made to the Personal Status Law on grounds they contradict Sharia. This would pertain to the reform in 2000 on *khula*, allowing a female spouse to initiate a divorce process without spousal consent, and reforms in 2004 such as the establishment of family courts and new child custody laws. For an up-to-date description of the Personal Status Law, see www2.gtz.de/dokumente/bib-2010/ gtz2010-0139en-faq-personal-status-law-egypt.pdf (last checked by the authors April 2014). See the Egypt Government's Services Portal for reference to the actual laws in Arabic: www.egypt.gov.eg/english/laws/ (last checked by the authors April 2014).

7. Based on CARE's women's empowerment framework, empowerment is conceptualised as the sum total of changes needed for a woman to realise her full human rights and involves the interplay of changes in agency (her own aspirations and capabilities), relations (the power relations through which she must negotiate her path), and structure (the environment that surrounds and conditions her choices). For more details on CARE's women's empowerment framework, see http://pqdl.care.org/sii/Pages/ Women's%20Empowerment%20SII%20Framework.aspx (last checked by the authors April 2014).

8. See note 7.

9. Shifting to a programme approach required a major shift in mindsets, organisational structure, how and what kind of funding is pursued, who CARE partners with, and how CARE works with different stakeholders. For example, one of the major changes needed for such a shift to work included CARE acting in close collaboration with others, particularly social movements and networks that can pursue rights-based agendas, and CARE seeing itself as one player amongst a multitude of other actors in society, many of whom are far better placed to push a social change agenda. This meant CARE had to embrace greater humility and consciousness to insert itself as a catalyst without always being in the lead and to act responsively when others take the lead. For more details of the changes that had to be pursued to make the programme shift, see *Brief No. 5: Designing Programmes* at: http://p-shift.care2share.wikispaces.net/ file/view/Brief%236_Designing%20programs_14%20Sept2009.pdf (last checked by the authors January 2014).

References

Anderson, Andrea A. (2004) *Theory of Change as a Tool for Strategic Planning: A Report on Early Experiences*, Washington, DC: The Aspen Institute, Roundtable on Community Change.

Weiss, Carol (1995) 'Nothing as practical as good theory: exploring theory-based evaluation for comprehensive community initiatives for children and families', in James Connell, Anne Kubisch, Lisbeth Schorr, and Carol Weiss (eds.) *New Approaches to Evaluating Community Initiatives Volume 1: Concepts, Methods, and Contexts*, Washington, DC: The Aspen Institute.

About the authors

Nidal Karim is Gender and Empowerment Impact Measurement Senior Advisor at CARE USA. Postal address: 151 Ellis Street NE, Atlanta, GA 30303-2440, USA. Email: nkarim@care.org

Mary Picard is an independent Evaluation Consultant. Postal address: 5718 Clark Street, Montreal, Quebec H2T 2V4, Canada. Email: picardm2002@yahoo.com

Sarah Gillingham is an independent Social Development Consultant. Postal address: 72 Marlborough Road, Grandpont, Oxford OX 1 4LR, UK. Email: sarah.gillingham@hotmail.co.uk

Leah Berkowitz is an independent Social Development Consultant. Postal address: 703 Hillside Village, 9th Street, Killarney, Johannesburg 2198, South Africa. Email: Leah.nchabeleng@gmail.com

CHAPTER 3

A review of approaches and methods to measure economic empowerment of women and girls

Paola Pereznieto and Georgia Taylor

Abstract

This chapter presents findings from a review of 70 evaluations of development interventions which had direct or indirect impacts on the economic empowerment of women and girls. We defined this as a process whereby women and girls experience transformation in power, agency, and economic advancement. The review distilled knowledge about monitoring, evaluation, and learning methods and approaches being used. It recommends the use of mixed (quantitative and qualitative) methods to assess economic empowerment comprehensively. It also explored the development and use of relevant indicators to measure economic empowerment of women and girls; the rigour with which methods are used; patterns in the use of different approaches for distinct thematic areas (micro-finance, social protection, fair trade, legal frameworks, and so on); and approaches used to bring out the voices of women, men, girls, and boys, among other key questions. It considered strengths, weaknesses, innovations, and challenges involved in evaluation and research approaches and methods based on primary data. The review, and this article, aim to inform agencies commissioning evaluations on how to ensure women's economic empowerment dimensions are captured; and to help those designing interventions to ensure these support positive transformation in the lives of women and girls.

Keywords: economic empowerment, gender, power, evaluation

Introduction

The economic empowerment of women and girls is understood by us to be a process whereby women and girls experience transformation in power and agency, as well as economic advancement. This chapter is based on a review of evaluations of development programmes and projects that directly or indirectly have an impact on women's and girls' economic empowerment (WGEE). The objective of the review was to provide information to improve the design and commissioning of evaluations to deliver stronger positive impacts across the different dimensions of WGEE. Overall, the aim was to inform agencies

http://dx.doi.org/10.3362/9781780447049.003

commissioning evaluations on how to ensure gender empowerment dimensions are captured; as well as those designing interventions on how to better foster the positive transformation of women and girls. The review was commissioned by the UK Government Department for International Development (DFID), and was carried out from March 2013 to March 2014.

The review was not based on primary data, but produced a meta-analysis based on many research and evaluation documents that did analyse primary data. The review explored strengths, weaknesses, innovations, challenges of evaluation and research approaches, and methods used in specific, grounded cases. The first stage identified 254 empirical evaluations and studies of mainstream and targeted interventions that measure or assess the effects of the intervention on WGEE. After a systematic screening process, a shortlist of 70 documents were analysed in detail by a panel of experts in order to distil knowledge about monitoring, evaluation, and learning methods and approaches being used to evaluate or analyse effects on WGEE.

The review explored a wide range of issues, including the use of quantitative and qualitative research methods in different types of development interventions with various aims. It also explored a range of key questions. These included the development and use of relevant indicators to measure economic empowerment of women and girls; the rigour with which methods are used; patterns in the use of different approaches for distinct thematic areas; and the development of legal frameworks around issues such as land and labour rights; and effective approaches that amplified the voices (that is, opinions and choices) of women and girls, whose voices are often absent in evaluation processes and reporting.

The review was wide in scope, analysing evaluations that included some measure of WGEE in one or more of the following thematic areas:

1. Financial services.
2. Business development services.
3. Skills training.
4. Asset provision (both financial and not financial).
5. Social protection.
6. Unions and fair employment.
7. Trade and access to markets.
8. Regulatory and legal frameworks.

This chapter shares some of the findings. We write it having developed the framework and methodology for the review, managed the review process, and undertaken the meta-analysis of expert reviews of the 70 shortlisted reports.

Defining and exploring WGEE

There is, of course, a wide literature focusing on women's empowerment as an economic, social and political process, and many writers have used a typology of power which identifies different forms of this, all of which are relevant in analyses of empowerment processes.[1] For the purpose of this review, we adapted aspects of this typology to shed light on WGEE specifically. We defined this as a process whereby women's and girls' lives are transformed from a situation where they have limited power and access to assets to a situation where they experience economic advancement, and their power and agency is enhanced (VeneKlasen and Miller 2002).

The four dimensions of power are referred to by us as 'change outcomes', and defined as follows:

1. *Power within*: the knowledge, individual capabilities, sense of entitlement, self-esteem, and self-belief to make changes in their lives, including learning skills to get a job or start an enterprise.
2. *Power to:* economic decision-making power within their household, community, and local economy (including markets), not just in areas that are traditionally regarded as women's realm, but extending to areas that are traditionally regarded as men's realm.
3. *Power over:* access to and control over financial, physical, and knowledge-based assets, including access to employment and income-generation activities.
4. *Power with:* the ability to organise with others to enhance economic activity and rights.

Empowerment is thus understood as a process of change that transforms women's and girls' lives in these four areas and interacts with resources (pre-conditions), agency (process), and achievements (outcomes) (Kabeer 1999). Naila Kabeer 's view of empowerment places economic empowerment in the spotlight as an essential underpinning of wider social and political empowerment of women, both as individuals and as a collective marginalised group. Empowerment will only be possible and sustainable if there are changes at different levels: within the individual (capability, knowledge, and self-esteem); in communities and institutions (including norms and behaviour); in available resources and economic opportunities; and in the wider political and legal environment (Golla *et al.* 2011).

Trends and gaps from the initial search

Based on the 254 studies included in the database, we can identify the following trends and gaps.

Trends

- Just under half (46 per cent) of the evaluations and studies focus primarily on financial services and their effects on WGEE. Within this thematic area, interventions supporting micro-credit and self-help groups (including savings and loans schemes) are commonly evaluated, but other areas such as micro-insurance and the use of new technologies (such as mobile phones) are less well explored.
- Interventions (particularly successful ones) promoting WGEE generally combine services across different thematic areas.

- There was a relatively even balance in terms of the methods used, with 30 per cent of the evaluations using quantitative methods, 38 per cent qualitative methods, and 28 per cent using mixed methods. Less than one in ten (9 per cent) used a different type of method or methods that were unclear. Among quantitative evaluations, the most common approaches to be used were randomised control trials (RCTs) and studies using quasi-experimental design.
- In geographical terms, around one-third of the reports covered interventions in South Asia (35 per cent), with a further one-third (30 per cent) focusing on interventions in sub-Saharan Africa.

Gaps

- Only one-fifth (21 per cent, or 55) of the evaluations and studies included in the database explored economic empowerment outcomes for adolescent girls. While these kinds of interventions have been increasing in recent years with initiatives such as the Girl Hub,[2] there are still few documented evaluations of their impacts.
- Most of the reports lacked age-disaggregated data, therefore failing to recognise the different experiences of girls and women during different stages of the life cycle.
- In terms of thematic areas, there were relatively few reports in three areas: legal and regulatory frameworks (two reports); unions and fair employment (six); and asset provision (four). This might be because few interventions in these areas have targeted women, reflecting a gender-blind approach; or it could be because a dearth of gender-disaggregated data in these areas does not allow for a differentiated analysis of the effects of these interventions on women's and men's economic empowerment.

An overview of the review methodology

The methodology used drew on and adapted systematic review principles,[3] in order to ensure a comprehensive search of the literature, and to identify as many relevant resources as possible. Since the objective of the review was to explore evaluation methodologies and approaches, rather than findings (which are generally the focus of reviews), the tools used at every stage were adapted to capture the information needed to answer the research questions.

The review process had three stages: an initial literature search, narrowing the field of inquiry, and review.

Initial literature search

The search strategy was designed to identify evidence and evaluations from across disciplines that report outcomes for WGEE. The search was largely Web-based and designed to cover both grey and academic literature, without privileging any particular discipline. The systematic search process used consistent inclusion criteria, search terms, coding, and search locations. A total of 382 papers were uploaded into the database for review. Only the 254 that reported empirical research (excluding systematic reviews, literature reviews, and theoretical papers) were subsequently analysed for quality in the next stage.

Narrowing the field of inquiry

To narrow down the field from the 254 empirical reports identified in the first stage, the research team devised a two-stage process using two different tools. The first 'basic scoring tool' captured the extent to which there was information on the methodological approaches used in the report. Reports that scored two or more points on that tool (160 of them) were then assessed using a purpose-designed 'quality assurance tool'. This tool gave a rapid assessment of quality, based on basic criteria set out for each methodological approach used. It provided a light-touch analysis through a rapid review of the documents, enabling further in-depth screening. Reports that scored two or more points on this second tool were considered for the final stage of the review. In total, 70 documents 'passed' the quality assurance test.

Review

Out of the 70 documents shortlisted, there was at least one in each of the eight thematic areas. They spanned a range of methodological approaches. Thirty-one used quantitative methods only, and a further 26 used a mix of both quantitative and qualitative methods, with 13 using qualitative methods alone.

Shortlisted reports were reviewed by a panel of four experts, using a review template that contained questions derived from evaluation best practice, as well as key resources on women's economic empowerment – for example, the Development Assistance Committee (DAC) criteria for evaluating development assistance,[4] Bond's quality of evaluation checklist, DFID's evaluation policy (DFID 2013), and Kabeer's (1999) paper on reflections on the measurement of women's empowerment. The purpose of the review template was to enable the expert panel to make a robust analysis of the quality of methodologies used, particularly in relation to their ability to capture relevant information about the effects of the intervention on WGEE. The individual reviews and the synthesis provided by each expert form the basis for our analysis, findings, and recommendations.

What makes a good-quality evaluation that effectively measures impact on WGEE?

This section analyses key dimensions of 'quality' in the approaches used by the 70 shortlisted evaluations or study documents that were reviewed by the expert panel. It gives examples from specific evaluations to illustrate strengths or weaknesses in relation to the quality criteria defined during the review phase. It draws largely on information from the expert reviews, and builds on insights derived from the meta-analysis of the set of reviews.

Applying a holistic approach to WGEE

According to the definition of WGEE used for this review, it is necessary for the intervention to result in some kind of transformational change on *women and girls' economic advancement and women's and girls' power and agency*, in addition to increasing income: we term that a 'holistic' approach.

Not all of the 70 shortlisted documents reflected such an approach; many looked at change in terms of economic advancement only. In cases where change in women's power and agency was assessed, it was common to limit this to decision-making power within the household. The quantitative studies were less likely to have a multi-dimensional and holistic view of women's economic empowerment, possibly because the types of indicators used tend to be more limited to changes in economic status, and do not always capture how and why changes happened to women and/or girls.

Evaluations that demonstrated a holistic approach to WGEE included those authored by Sally Baden (2013), on Oxfam work, Supriya Garikipati (2008), Sirojuddin Arif *et al.* (2010), on Overseas Development Institute (ODI) work, and Nicola Jones and Mohammed Shaheen (2012), on ODI work. However, there are varying levels of sophistication of the WGEE frameworks used. At the very minimum, the evaluation would measure changes in the individual's decision-making power within the household as a measure of women's agency. *The lack of measurement of change in norms and attitudes* was generally not done at the institutional level and at the level of the legal and policy-enabling environment.

Building an evaluation team with gender expertise

The review found that evaluation teams with gender experts or expertise presented better quality analysis in relation to WGEE – a finding that perhaps is not so surprising to gender and development practitioners. In addition, gender expertise ensured integration of gender concerns into research methodology.

Preparing for the evaluation and understanding the context

Good-quality evaluations in the review always contained a good analysis of the social and economic context, including a strong gender analysis. If context analysis is done sufficiently well, it will enable a relevant theory of change and an evaluation methodology that takes into account the context. Good context analysis presented market and economic context, political and institutional context, gender analysis including data on the gender division of labour, roles and power relations, and information on wider processes of economic, social, and political change at household, community, and institutional levels.

Gender analysis is key to good context analysis. This is essential for good-quality evaluations, and our findings bore this out. Fewer than 25 per cent of the reports reviewed included a strong gender analysis. Gender differences, gender-related norms and behaviours, gender roles, and gender relations differ in every context, and assumptions should not be made when designing an evaluation. In some cases, an evaluation did aim to measure women's economic empowerment but there was a lack of understanding of the importance of the multiple gender inequality dimensions present, and how they related to the intervention's achievements, and its evaluation.

Most of the highest-scoring evaluations and studies had a well-articulated theoretical framework and/or theory of change. This enabled the evaluators to demonstrate where and how change would happen as a result of the intervention – and thereby to frame their evaluation around that change process. The best theories of change showed dynamic and multi-faceted change processes that reflected transformational changes in women's agency and economic advancement, and the relationship between them.

A useful theory of change can be seen in the evaluation of Henny Slegh *et al.* (2013) of a pilot project in Rwanda that targeted male partners of women involved in a CARE-funded microfinance scheme so as to counter gender norms, power dynamics, and gender-based violence. The report found that women participants in micro-credit programmes need to be supported by improved and better programming which engages with men in deliberate and structured ways, including promoting greater male involvement in care work and that in some settings, solely focusing on women may lead to negative effects for women, both in the short and long term. The theory of change employed situates the pilot project within broader literature on the multiple spill-over effects of women's economic empowerment on their individual social well-being and on familial well-being. But they note that this positive relationship cannot be assumed and is, in part, dependent on men's reactions to women's changing roles and status.

Methodology and indicators

The review found that mixed-methods evaluations were the most effective in terms of measuring change and outcomes, and also provided good material for learning and improving future project design. This finding is in line with feminist literature on research methods (Oakley 2000). A good mixed-methods approach means that qualitative and quantitative data can complement each other, so that the whole is more than the sum of its parts. It also allows for effective triangulation[5] of data. In low-resource cases and when mixed methods is not feasible, qualitative or quantitative data alone would be useful as long as the evaluation design was robust and includes 'holistic' indicators for gender economic empowerment, has a solid theory of change around transformational impacts of the evaluation on women and/or girls, and where a gender expert supports the research design and/or analysis of findings to ensure important aspects are analysed. There are complementary roles of both kinds of methods:

- *Quantitative* methodologies tended to be used to demonstrate that: (1) change had taken place; (2) the intervention caused the change to take place (*causality*); and (3) the findings can be generalised across a population group (in the case of representative samples).
- *Qualitative* methodologies were most commonly used for: (1) context analysis to design sampling and tools; (2) conducting participatory activities to identify indicators of change; (3) establishing how the change takes place; (4) understanding *why* change happens (or does not happen); (5) researching how people understand and describe that change; and (6) identifying unintended changes or impacts.

Sequencing of quantitative and qualitative data collection was relative to the particular role each method played in the overall evaluation. However, in the reports reviewed it was rare to see a good-quality explanation of why mixed methods had been chosen, and how a particular sequence had been decided.

Multiple sources of data were important for triangulation in cases where there was no baseline. Evaluations were generally scored higher if the analysis in a mixed-methods approach used both the quantitative and qualitative data to complement and reinforce each other. However, thorough triangulation in mixed-methods evaluations was rare; many had separate and distinct sections for the qualitative and quantitative aspects, which in some cases did not reference each other.

Funding appeared to be lower for qualitative evaluations. A large number of those reviewed (or parts of them) had limited scope and reach, with small samples. This suggests a lack of value and funding attached to qualitative methods. In many of the studies reviewed, it is unlikely that the point of data saturation was reached.

For *measures of change*, the choice of dependent variables for quantitative analysis is vitally important for a good-quality assessment of change in WGEE.

In many cases, evaluations were measuring progress against a pre-agreed set of indicators that appeared to be at output level only, with no analysis of unexpected or wider changes that might have taken place. Measurement of change at outcome or impact level required a set of indicators that (given the context) adequately measured transformational change on women's and girls' economic advancement and power and agency.

The reviews identified that evaluation teams and researchers often make underlying assumptions about gender roles and relations, and women's activities, and use stereotypes. This can limit the level of analysis, for example leading to women and men being asked questions based on misconceptions:

- *Type of expenditure:* Women may only be asked about expenditure on household items or child-related expenditure, whereas men are asked about recreation and other activities. This reinforces the stereotype that women are supposed to be responsible for household and child-related expenditure, and may limit investigation into changes that could be taking place. It also negates the possibility that men may also have a responsibility for household expenditure.

- *Type of decisions:* Women are typically asked about who makes decisions about issues that are relevant to the division of household labour (that is, who decides how women's and children's time is allocated), but seldom asked about other critical areas of life such as decisions about who participates in community or civic events, how women's time is allocated to activities outside the household (labour or social), and the like. Only rarely may questions be asked about joint decision-making, with researchers tending to frame their questions as 'either/or' (e.g. are household decisions made by men or women?). In many cases, joint decision-making is the norm in many decision-making spheres. Even when this is revealed it is rare to see an analysis that explores the relative power balance between men and women who are making decisions together. In general, this level of detail was missing from the evaluations

- *Type of economic activities:* Assumptions may be made about women being home-based, or economically active only in certain sectors, so that their involvement in other sectors is not considered. Considerations must also be made of unpaid care work or subsistence work which changes women's workload dramatically and completely affects their engagement or non-engagement with paid work.

Evaluations that scored well used a multi-dimensional range of indicators to measure women's and girls' economic advancement and changes in their power and agency. The most innovative studies used unique power variables that captured concepts of economic empowerment that one might not normally consider, such as whether a young girl was less likely to have unwanted sex. An example is a study by Oriana Bandiera *et al.* (2012), focusing on the Empowerment and Livelihood for Adolescents (ELA) programme – implemented by the non-government organisation BRAC Uganda – which is designed to improve the cognitive and non-cognitive skills of adolescent girls. The study aims to look at how this intervention uses a dual-pronged approach, aiming to affect adolescent girls' economic prospects, sexual behaviour, and life attitudes. The dual-pronged approach aims to (1) build life skills to build knowledge and reduce risky forms of behaviour, and (2) provide vocational training aiming to enable girls to establish small-scale enterprises.

The choice of what variables to use will obviously be context-specific; and ideally indicators will be defined in a participative way with and by women and men. As this is often not possible, the review highlights a number of innovative variables that could be considered for use. These draw on generic elements of an experience of lack of power – lack of control over resources being a foundational element – which echo the generic model of empowerment laid out by Naila Kabeer. The ways in which these generic elements are manifested in a particular context and for a particular woman will vary.

A good example of indicators used can be found in Ranjula Bali Swain and Wallentin's (2007) study of whether microfinance empowers self-help groups in India. This study used indicators that included: women's primary activity; access to independent savings; hypothetical response to possible verbal, physical, and emotional abuse; awareness of rights; and political activity. These indicators go beyond traditional 'decision-making' indicators and encompass other areas of women's control over their lives that are appropriate for the economic empowerment topic and context under evaluation.

An example of how indicators can be made relevant to particular women in a specific context through participatory planning methods is offered by the study of Syed Hashemi *et al.* (1996) on women's rural credit programmes in Bangladesh which used eight indicators (with sub-variables and weighting for each) that were developed through extensive observation, personal interviews with respondents in the ethnographic study villages and with credit programme staff, as well as from basic survey data. Responses were consolidated into the following eight indicators: mobility; economic security; ability to make small purchases; ability to make larger purchases; involvement in major decisions; relative freedom from domination by the family; political and legal awareness; and participation in public protests and political campaigning. There was also a composite empowerment indicator by which a woman was classified as empowered if she had a positive score on five or more of the main eight indicators. In creating the empowerment indicators, the authors intentionally included a variety of specific actions or items in each one and made a minimal use of weights. All the operational measures of empowerment in the analysis reduce empowerment to dichotomous variables (empowered versus un-empowered). The cut-off points were based on percentage distributions for each dimension, with those classified as 'empowered' being around the 25th or 30th percentile for most dimensions.

Hardly any of the reviewed documents had included a list and description of the complete set of evaluation tools used, either in the main report or in annexes; in some cases, sets of questions were included in footnotes (an example is Oriana Bandiera *et al.* 2012, in a study of BRAC Uganda's ELA programme, discussed above). Some reviews with good-quality methodology had poor design and implementation of instruments, which led to poor-quality data and weak analysis. Data collection methods sections in the reports reviewed rarely discussed gender issues with respect to methodology and enumerators/interviewers.

Involvement of men, boys, and young women and girls in the evaluation

Many of the evaluations reviewed did not conduct interviews, surveys, or focus group discussions with men and/or young men, unless the project was specifically targeted at men as well. It could be argued that it is impossible to measure women's economic empowerment unless men's attitudes and behaviours are also taken into account. It is also true that issues including the relative contribution and therefore significance of women's income cannot be discerned – even though these issues are important to the question of empowerment within marriage and the family – without research into men's economic role within the household. This can be questioned in interviews with women but triangulation and direct involvement of men in interviews is likely to improve the reliability of data. The engagement of men was seen as critical in gaining acceptance for the strategies chosen to improve women's economic empowerment. Some of the evaluations had a general sample with men and women, but with no disaggregation of results, so women's empowerment was not easy to identify.

There were very few evaluations of interventions targeting girls' or young people's economic empowerment. Reports were excluded because they were either poor quality and/or lacked detail. In the other evaluations, lack of age-disaggregated data meant that impact on women and girls was not separated out, even though there are many young women and girls who are married and may form an important part of a sample. There was no evidence of differentiated approaches being used.

Inadequacies in the survey or interview methodology

Though women's voices were captured in most evaluations, data analysis and presentation of quantitative evaluations hardly ever reported women's voices verbatim. This is a shame since direct quotations not only enable a better sense of women's own perceptions and hence more accurate data, but also women's voices convey findings more powerfully.

The review showed that questions are sometimes based on recall, with insufficient triangulation to back up the findings. Factual information may not be remembered accurately. Most of the expert reviewers agreed that recall is subjective and can be unreliable, so other data sources are needed.

Recommendations

The main justification for diverting funds to evaluation from implementation of a WGEE intervention is to yield practical recommendations for increasing its contribution to women's economic empowerment and for learning within the sector. With this in mind, recommendations have been made here to improve evaluation quality and learning potential.

Overarching recommendations

Ideally, evaluation frameworks should be designed at the project design stage and should have a methodology and indicators that are relevant to the project's theory of change, and should include a baseline.

Clarity of purpose and a strategy for how the evaluation findings will be used are essential from the outset.

Different types of interventions may require different evaluation approaches but should be taken to avoid 'ticking the gender box' with an approach and analysis that is not sufficiently in-depth. It is important to ensure that projects are built around a full understanding of the gender context, even where a gender component appears to be an afterthought.

When designing mixed-methods evaluations, it is important to ensure that both the quantitative and qualitative components are well designed and able to complement each other, either by sequencing findings from one to inform the design of the other, or by ensuring that each approach collects complementary data.

The review identified very few evaluations and studies that looked at the economic empowerment of adolescent girls, despite a growing interest in this field. This implies a need for such interventions, but also for stronger evaluations and research in this area. Such interventions provide an opportunity to engage adolescent girls, and thus also present an opportunity to assess impact on this important age group.

Reports should include summary diagrams or tables. Excellent material and findings can be buried if they are not then translated into easily accessible formats.

It is useful if evaluations are part of a clear plan for dissemination of findings to deliver on the evaluation's purpose if this is to include learning and better implementation of the intervention in question (and similar interventions). Ideally, evaluation findings should be shared with research participants.

The report's recommendations should provide clear guidance for how to enhance impact on WGEE – and this should include policy implications. Policy recommendations could be enriched by drawing on evaluators' broader experience and knowledge in the field, not only the findings that come directly from the specific piece of research.

Build a team that has sufficient gender expertise and involve it from the beginning in evaluation design and context analysis

Evaluations should aim to include experts with solid experience and expertise in gender and economic empowerment/enterprise. Ideally, gender experts should know the technical area of the intervention being evaluated. If evaluators have expertise in a particular technical area but are not gender experts, the team's skills should be complemented with at least one gender expert, participating in the evaluation design stage but ideally also the data analysis stage.

Data collection with women, particularly on intra-household dimensions of economic empowerment, is best done by other women wherever possible in order to facilitate open discussions of constraints to women's agency. Where this is not possible due to the composition of the fieldwork team, the evaluation or study report should state that this was the case and note any possible response biases this might have caused.

Undertake context analysis that has a full gender analysis, and ensure there is a theory of change that describes transformational change in women's and girls' economic advancement and power and agency

Exploring women's economic empowerment (and the impact of any intervention) relies on a thorough context and problem analysis. The context analysis should cover gender equality and the economic, political, and technical context, so that the limitations of gender equality and its impact on women are fully understood.

Evaluation teams should not make assumptions about gender behaviour across contexts or allow underlying cultural and gender stereotypes held by the evaluation team, the data collection teams, or national partners to act as a barrier to good data collection and analysis, as this may ultimately limit the validity of the evaluation findings.

There should be a discussion of how political, economic, or natural situations and crises may have influenced the findings of the evaluation, particularly about WGEE.

It is essential to have a (explicit or implicit) theory of change that depicts the expected change processes, and guides the research questions and formation of indicators. This should include how transformational change is expected to take place in the short term, medium term and long term, and should cover changes in women's economic situation *and* agency.

Depending on the context analysis and the scope of the intervention being evaluated, the theory of change should show gender-related change expected at different levels: individuals, communities, institutions, and the legal and policy environment.

Use mixed methods effectively and ensure that indicators adequately measure transformational change

A set of minimum evaluation methodology standards would be a good way of ensuring quality. These could include some or all of the following.

Evaluations should provide a full explanation of the methodology and indicators used, including information about why certain choices were made and the limitations of the chosen methodology.

Mixed-methods evaluations should be used for WGEE interventions where possible. The evaluation should aim to establish whether change took place and what caused it, through quantitative analysis. However, qualitative information will be needed to understand the process of change, and how implementation has been experienced by individuals, as well as to uncover any unintended impacts or changes and other factors that may have influenced change. This is especially important for WGEE projects as changes in norms, attitudes, and behaviours are difficult to understand fully with quantitative data alone.

RCTs are generally considered the 'gold standard' of research methodology for evaluating impact, proving causality, and generalising findings. However, when resources or technical expertise are insufficient to do a comprehensive and statistically sound quantitative evaluation, other methods should be considered. Information can be more cheaply collected through use of good qualitative or participatory methods, together with a simple survey focusing on specific issues arising. Quasi-experimental design, drawing on propensity score matching (PSM) or difference in difference (DD) are a good alternative when RCTs are technically not feasible, because there can be no randomisation (e.g. when the evaluation is done after the intervention has been implemented), if robustly designed and implemented. They are best complemented by qualitative data.[6]

When using qualitative methods, it is important to include quotes from in-depth interviews and case studies as these add legitimacy to the findings and help to bring the issues alive for the reader.

Indicators and tools to be used in the evaluation should be based on local knowledge. Conduct prior and follow-up participatory and/or qualitative research to identify appropriate local indicators and ways of wording questions so that they are likely to be clearly understood and taken seriously by interviewees and thus encourage the most reliable responses.

Indicators should include measurement of the following:

- transformational change in women's economic advancement and agency;
- attitudes, norms, and behaviours of women and men;
- change in gender mainstreaming and attitudes in institutions;
- gender differences in empowerment between women and men to increase local relevance;
- changes in men's and women's social capital, economic autonomy, and political participation;
- rights of women in enterprise;
- effects of the wider market, value chain, and employment, as all of these will affect women's economic advancement and empowerment.

Ensure that sampling selections are explained and justified, and that data are disaggregated fully by age, sex, and other relevant groups

The sample should include women and men, and, where appropriate, girls and boys – even if the intervention is targeted at women and girls only. Evaluators and researchers should analyse the difference, the co-dependence between the groups, the positive outcomes, and relationships between men and women – not just the outcomes for women.

Evaluations should differentiate between women of different ages and their stages in the life cycle, as well as women from different backgrounds, even if the conclusion is that these different groups of women need something apart from the project activities; findings might yield important information about complementary services that would need to be put in place to maximise impact.

Appropriate tools should be designed for different study participants and provided in full in the research report

Evaluators should ensure that the evaluation/study tools are available in the final report (as an annex) for transparency and replicability.

The team should design appropriate tools and data collection methods for young people and different population groups in the sample. This is particularly important when collecting sensitive data from adolescent girls and boys. Participatory tools can work well with this cohort.

In order to demonstrate effect and especially impact in the absence of baseline data, there should be greater use of *historical tools* – e.g. life histories, generational comparisons, community histories.

Notes

1. The four dimensions of power referred to here have been developed and adapted from earlier work which is well-referenced in the literature. For example, the concept of 'power-over' particular individuals or groups was first conceptualised by Stephen Lukes (1974) as structural domination – a quite different usage from the positive sense in which it is used in this typology used in the review. The other dimensions of power are used widely in writings on women, power, and development (e.g. Kabeer 1994; Rowlands 1997; Townsend *et al.* 1999).
2. A joint initiative between DFID and the Nike Foundation.
3. Although first applied in the medical sciences in the 1970s, systematic reviews have been recently, and increasingly, used in the field of international development to examine the impacts of a range of development and humanitarian interventions. Systematic reviews are a rigorous and transparent form of literature review. Described as 'the most reliable and comprehensive statement about what works', systematic reviews involve identifying, synthesising, and assessing all available evidence, quantitative and/or qualitative, in order to generate a robust, empirically derived answer to a focused research question (Mallett *et al.* 2012); also 'DAC Criteria for Evaluating Development Assistance', www.oecd.org/dac/evaluation/daccriteriaforevaluatingdevelopmentassistance.htm (last checked by the authors May 2014).
4. The four experts on the panel have significant experience of issues of gender equity and women's empowerment, as well as robust knowledge of quantitative and qualitative research methodologies. Nevertheless, when assessing the quality of a report, panel members were influenced by their

individual expertise, knowledge base, and methodological preference. This review presents a balanced analysis based on careful reading of all the individual reviews and the analytical syntheses prepared by each expert.

5. Triangulation refers to the use of more than one approach to the investigation of a research question in order to enhance confidence in the ensuing findings. Since much social research is founded on the use of a single research method and as such may suffer from limitations associated with that method or from the specific application of it, triangulation offers the prospect of enhanced confidence.

6. Impact evaluations estimate programme effectiveness usually by comparing outcomes of those (individuals, communities, schools, etc.) who participated in the programme against those who did not participate. The key challenge in impact evaluation is finding a group of people who did not participate, but closely resemble the participants had those participants not received the programme. Measuring outcomes in this comparison group is as close as we can get to measuring 'how participants would have been otherwise'. There are many methods of creating a comparison group. Some methods are better than others. From a quantitative research perspective, all else equal, randomised evaluations (or randomised control trials) are the most effective. They generate a statistically identical comparison group, and therefore produce the most accurate (unbiased) results. There are 'quasi=experimental' methods that can be used when randomisation is not possible, and a different control group needs to be identified. Some of the common techniques used by this approach include PSM and DD. A detailed explanation of when different quasi-experimental methods should be used is found at: www.povertyaction lab.org/sites/default/files/documents/Experimental%20Methodology%20 Table.pdf (last checked by the authors May 2014).

References

Arif, Sirojuddin, Muhammad Syukri, Rebecca Holmes, and Vita Febriany (2010) *Gendered Risks, Poverty, and Vulnerability: Case Study of the Raskin Food Subsidy Programme in Indonesia*, London: Overseas Development Institute.

Baden, Sally (2013) *Women's Collective Action: Unlocking the Potential of Agricultural Markets*, Oxford: Oxfam GB for Oxfam International.

Bandiera, Oriana, Niklas Buehren, Robin Burgess, Markus Goldstein, Selim Gulesci, Imran Rasul, and Munshi Sulaiman (2012) *Empowering Adolescent Girls: Evidence from a Randomized Control Trial in Uganda*, London School of Economics, http://econ.lse.ac.uk/staff/rburgess/wp/ELA.pdf (last checked by the authors May 2014).

Department for International Development (2013) 'International Development Evaluation Policy', May 2013, London: DfID.

Garikipati, Supriya (2008) 'The impact of lending to women on household vulnerability and women's empowerment: evidence from India', *World Development* 36(12): 2620–42.

Golla, Anne Marie, Anju Malhotra, Priya Nanda, and Rekha Mehra (2011) *Understanding and Measuring Women's Economic Empowerment. Definition,*

Framework and Indicators, Washington, DC: International Centre for Research on Women.

Hashemi, Syed, Sydney Ruth Schuler, and Ann P. Riley (1996) 'Rural credit programs and women's empowerment in Bangladesh', *World Development* 24(4): 635–53.

Jones, Nicola and Mohammed Shaheen (2012) *Transforming Cash Transfers: Beneficiary and Community Perspectives of the Palestinian National Cash Transfer Programme*, London: Overseas Development Institute.

Kabeer, Naila (1994) *Reversed Realities: Gender Hierarchies in Development Thought*, London and New York: Verso.

Kabeer, Naila (1999) 'Resources, agency, achievements: reflections on the measurement of women's empowerment', *Development and Change* 30(3): 435–64.

Lukes, Stephen (1974) *Power: A Radical View*, London: Macmillan.

Mallett, Richard, Jessica Hagen-Zanker, Rachel Slater, and Maren Duvendack (2012) 'The benefits and challenges of using systematic reviews in international development research', *Journal of Development Effectiveness* 4(3): 445–55.

Oakley, Ann (2000) *Experiments in Knowing: Gender and method in the social sciences*, Cambridge: Polity Press.

Rowlands, Jo (1997) *Questioning Empowerment: Working with Women in Honduras*, Oxford: Oxfam GB.

Slegh, Henny, Gary Barker, Augustin Kimonyo, P. Ndolimana and Matt Bannerman (2013) '"I can do women's work": reflections on engaging men as allies in women's economic empowerment in Rwanda', *Gender & Development* 21(1): 15–30.

Swain, Ranjula Bali and Fan Yang Wallentin (2007) *Does Microfinance Empower Women?* Evidence from Self Help Groups in India, Working Paper No. 2007:24, Uppsala: Uppsala University, Department of Economics.

Townsend, Janet, Emma Zapata, Jo Rowlands, Pilar Alberti and Marta Mercado (1999) *Women and Power: Fighting Patriarchies & Poverty*, London: Zed Books.

VeneKlasen, Lisa and Valerie Miller (2002) *A New Weave of Power, People and Politics: The Action Guide for Advocacy and Citizen Participation*, Bourton on Dunsmore, Rugby: Practical Action Publishing.

About the authors

Paola Pereznieto is a Research Associate in the Social Development Programme, Overseas Development Institute. Postal address: 203 Blackfriars Road, London SE1 8NJ, UK, as well as a freelance consultant. Email: p.pereznieto@odi.org.uk

Georgia Taylor is a freelance consultant and a director of WISE Development, Central Hall Westminster. Postal address: Storey's Gate, London SW1H 9NH, UK. Email: georgiat@btinternet.com

CHAPTER 4

Still learning: a critical reflection on three years of measuring women's empowerment in Oxfam

David Bishop and Kimberly Bowman

Abstract

In 2011, as part of a broader effort to understand organisational effectiveness, a team within Oxfam GB began implementing impact evaluations on a small sample of projects largely focused on women's empowerment. The resulting 'Women's Empowerment Effectiveness Reviews' employ a quasi-experimental evaluation design, and have been undertaken in more than a dozen sites over three years. This chapter briefly presents the Women's Empowerment Effectiveness Reviews and their short history, then focuses on five key areas where the approach has presented limitations. Acknowledging that there remains room for improvement, the project has also been a major step forward for Oxfam's monitoring, evaluation, and learning practice. Through this critical reflection, we aim to share some learning to date.

Keywords: impact evaluation, empowerment, women's rights

Introduction

Seen through the eyes of monitoring and evaluation specialists, 'women's empowerment' is both an inspiring and challenging concept. It is inspiring to consider the potential for evaluation to illustrate and support truly transformational but often hidden changes: women claiming and enjoying their rights, being able to make decisions about the direction of their lives, or beginning to access power denied to them. Empowerment is also deeply challenging from a measurement perspective – an abstract and contested concept boasting a range of sometimes-dry definitions. There are those who argue that any attempt to measure it is sure to disappoint someone, and certainly fail to capture its transformational elements. That said, evaluation advisors with Oxfam are committed to 'putting women's rights at the heart of everything we do'.[1]

In 2010, Oxfam GB's senior leadership team requested that the organisation's Programme Performance & Accountability Team develop a framework for understanding organisational performance.[2] Oxfam's programming is broad and diverse, but the leadership specifically instructed that an assessment of

http://dx.doi.org/10.3362/9781780447049.004

the effectiveness of programming aimed at empowering women be included within this framework.

Oxfam and others have previously discussed different design choices for organisational performance frameworks on the whole. Establishing such a framework is particularly tricky for organisations with very diverse or 'hard to measure' programming. Oxfam recognises that transformational empowerment involves the realisation of economic, social, and political rights that are often interdependent and reinforcing, and which women experience in different ways within personal, household, local community, and broader political spheres. Oxfam's programming often involves livelihoods approaches, using economic changes as an entry point to prompt other changes (including empowerment) in the social and political spheres.

The focus on women's rights and gender justice in Oxfam's work results from the understanding that gender inequality is both a cause of, and perpetuated by, poverty and suffering. Efforts to support women's empowerment cut across Oxfam's programming – from engaging men in ending violence against women to work on women's rights legislation at national and international levels.

Our understanding and definition of women's empowerment as a construct should necessarily drive the measurement approach. Academics, feminist activists, and gender and development practitioners have previously identified many challenges to measuring women's empowerment (notably Kabeer 1999); many of which have been borne out as Oxfam attempted to design a practical evaluation approach to measure changes in women's empowerment. First, definitional issues required resolution: should we define empowerment as a process, or as a state of being? As something that could be externally defined, or something which the person we are hoping to support in her empowerment process can – and should – judge for herself? Is empowerment a coherent but abstract concept (e.g. the ability to make strategic life choices), or something that can be judged by assessing a range of characteristics or smaller component parts?

Organisational requirements have also imposed challenges. Oxfam GB was seeking an approach that could be applied appropriately in a range of contexts, while also producing data that could be aggregated at cross-national or 'global' level, for use by senior managers and for donor reporting.[3] The aggregation demand posed considerable challenges for evaluating an area of programming where context is so critical. Economic, social, and political marginalisation of women plays out in radically different ways in different contexts, resulting in a wide variety of norms and practices which disempower women. Further complexity is added from the multiple other identities of women which create an experience of intersectional inequality which varies from woman to woman. Importantly, as readers will appreciate, change itself is extremely complex and messy to chart, particularly in relation to tracking shifts in power relations. Meaningful change can be slow, hidden, 'two-steps-forward-one-stepback'[4] – and like all issues of power, women's empowerment is intensely personal and politicised. With all this in mind, we needed an approach that was sufficiently precise to detect small changes which can accrue over time, while also appreciating the complexity of the issue to be measured.

Finally and crucially, limitations in programme monitoring and evaluation practice in some Oxfam projects reviewed meant that consistent and high-quality baseline information was not available. Therefore these impact evaluations have hitherto been exclusively ex-post, relying on attempts to recall baseline status by survey respondents.

This chapter aims to be a critical self-examination of our efforts to respond to these challenges, through developing and undertaking a series of impact evaluations on women's empowerment interventions, which were catalysed by Oxfam's implementation of its 'Global Performance Framework' in 2010. The chapter draws upon more than a dozen impact evaluations carried out in Asia, Latin America, the Middle East, Eastern Europe, and Africa between 2011 and 2013. These evaluations – called Women's Empowerment Effectiveness Reviews – were led by members of Oxfam GB's Programme Performance & Accountability Team, in collaboration with country programme teams, global and regional advisors, local non-government organisations (NGOs) working in partnership with Oxfam, and external consultants and enumerators.[5]

As 'large *n*' (i.e. large sample) impact evaluations, the Women's Empowerment Effectiveness Reviews have had, as their focus, programming that is delivered primarily at the household or community level. Perhaps predictably – bearing in mind the anti-poverty focus of many development interventions at household and community levels – the majority of programmes reviewed to date have been focused on women's economic empowerment through community-based livelihoods interventions. Interventions that aim to challenge unequal gender power relations at other levels, such as national or international policy work, are covered by a different, qualitative, evaluation design.

We believe that Oxfam is sincere about wanting to understand better its contribution to changes in women's lives and in gender power relations. We believe that these evaluations have been a major step forward – though the approach has involved trade-offs, and there remains room for improvement. Our aim now is to share our learning at this stage of the process.

In the rest of this chapter, we will briefly present the Women's Empowerment Effectiveness Reviews, relate their short history, and then focus on five key areas where the tool has presented difficult limitations. We hope that through sharing Oxfam's practical experience – warts and all – we can make a meaningful contribution to the community of funders, evaluators, and development practitioners who see quality evaluation as a tool to support women's empowerment.

Measuring women's empowerment – the tool

As stated above, the catalyst for developing a common approach to measuring the effectiveness of women's empowerment programming – in the form of the Women's Empowerment Index – was Oxfam's implementation of its 'Global

Performance Framework' in 2010. The framework was designed to help the organisation better understand and demonstrate the scale and effectiveness of its work. Different NGOs have used a range of different approaches to respond to the 'results agenda', to drive improvements in organisational learning and to be more accountable to partners, allies, and donors.

Describing the complete performance framework is beyond the scope of this chapter (for more details, see Hughes and Hutchings 2011), but a large component of the framework involves impact evaluations which assess whether Oxfam's interventions have contributed to positive change in different thematic outcome areas. As we mentioned earlier, Oxfam is an organisation that strives to put women's rights at the heart of everything we do, and one of the key thematic areas Oxfam's senior leadership chose to review was the impact of its interventions on women's empowerment. A 'global outcome indicator' was proposed, namely 'the percentage of supported women demonstrating significantly greater involvement in household decision-making and influencing affairs at the community level', to which each impact evaluation in this theme would report.

This global outcome indicator therefore provided the initial focus for the measurement approach, but – as we go on here to discuss – the approach has since expanded to include further dimensions of empowerment. The nature of this indicator is important, as it determined the nature of project interventions which would be evaluated; how 'empowerment' was defined and assessed in these evaluations; and, to a large degree, the evaluation method applied.

The impact evaluations involve the application of quasi-experimental methods to evaluate a random sample of interventions primarily implemented at a household or community level. These methods involve the use of household-level surveys with people participating in an Oxfam-supported project, as well as with a comparable population in areas where the project is not active. Through the use of statistical analysis methods (multi-variable regression and propensity-score matching),[6] evaluators are able to compare these two groups, and discern where there is evidence of project impact on key empowerment or livelihood outcomes. Evaluations are designed by a team of three specialists and implemented with and through country programme teams and partners with the assistance of local consultants and survey staff.

The approach was designed to meet demands – from both internal and external stakeholders – for impact evaluations that were substantially more focused and rigorous than Oxfam's average, of projects that usually had no formal baseline and often limited monitoring data. Budget was also a factor in determining approach: with a budget of approximately £20,000 (including staff time) per effectiveness review and a total of 12 'large *n*' studies conducted by this team of three each year, the size of the surveyed population is limited. The evaluations were conducted at the end of the project, and as such, experimental evaluation approaches which rely on randomising participants into an intervention at the start of the project, for example, randomised control trials, were not an option.

Year one (2011/12)

The first set of Women's Empowerment Effectiveness Reviews focused on aspects considered by Oxfam's evaluation team and thematic specialist staff to be most important and relevant to the projects selected for review. A questionnaire was administered by survey staff to women in households reached by the project activities. It was also administered to others in comparison communities, which had not participated in the projects. It asked respondents about two sets of issues: first, their involvement in several aspects of household decision-making, such as decisions regarding the purchase of new assets, or choices related to children's education or family planning, and second, their participation in community-level leadership and decision-making. Beyond these two main areas of decision-making, further questions covered issues pertaining to self-confidence, and women's ownership of assets – including both those used in production, and also other high-value assets like jewellery or a television, which can potentially be sold to raise capital.

This questionnaire was implemented across the first set of three Women's Empowerment Effectiveness Reviews in 2011/12. While the dimensions of empowerment covered by these first-generation reviews were quite limited, and the questionnaire implemented quite inflexibly across the different country contexts, some interesting top-level findings emerged. For example, in each of the three projects under review, there was evidence that some women participants in the project were more likely to have the opportunity and feel able to influence affairs in their community. In contrast, none of the reviews found clear evidence of women's increased involvement in key aspects of household decision-making.

These may not be particularly surprising results, given that several of the projects under review were actively establishing women's farmer groups or co-operatives, or providing community-level training on women's rights, which may have directly impacted on the respondent's opportunity to contribute to community-level decision-making even in the short or medium term. Also, patterns of household-level decision-making are arguably more connected to cultural norms and are perhaps more likely to take longer to change. However, it is important to note that having such findings – especially derived from a more rigorous evaluative approach – provided opportunity to have productive discussions on the issues raised by the reviews, and helped get traction from project teams, policy advisers, and senior management to explore the concept of empowerment in greater depth and detail.

Years two and three (2012/13 and 2013/14)

As Oxfam embarked on the second year of reviews in 2012/13, the team was keen to learn both from the experience of the first year of implementation, as well as from the experience of other organisations who were similarly trying to tackle the definition and measurement of women's empowerment. In trying to come up with a framework for measuring another 'hard-to-measure' concept – resilience – Oxfam had the opportunity to learn from the experience of the Oxford Poverty and Human Development Initiative (OPHI) and its work to develop a multi-dimensional approach to measuring poverty.

Alongside its multi-dimensional poverty analysis work, OPHI has also joined with the International Food Policy and Research Institute (IFPRI) to develop a multi-dimensional tool to measure women's empowerment in agriculture. The Women's Empowerment in Agriculture Index, which resulted, is a composite measure which is comprised of several 'domains' considered important to the empowerment of women farmers, including involvement in decisions about agricultural production, decision-making power over productive resources, control over use of income, leadership in the community, and time use (Alkire *et al.* 2012). One or more indicators is connected to each of these domains, and information on each is captured through household surveys.

Building on this approach, the effectiveness review team defined four domains, together with ten constituent characteristics assessed to be most appropriate to the broader approaches and context in which Oxfam works. Table 4.1 illustrates these.

The questionnaire used in year one was modified in order to capture information on each of the ten characteristics, and in the analysis stage we employed the OPHI approach to aggregate this information into one overall 'empowerment score' for each female respondent.[7] As in 2011/12, surveys were carried out with both project participants and with appropriate comparison respondents.

Using this new method, evaluators are able to determine whether there was evidence that the project had affected overall empowerment – as measured by this framework – as well as what changes had occurred in relation to the various domains and characteristics included in the framework.

Table 4.1 Dimensions of empowerment – year two

Dimension	Characteristics
Household decision-making	Input in productive decisions
	Input to other household decisions
Control over resources	Access to credit
	Ownership of strategic assets
Public engagement	Community influencing
	Group involvement
Self-perception	Self-efficacy
	Attitude to sharing household duties
	Attitude to women's rights
	Attitude to position of women

For example, in looking at the underlying detail from one of the reviews in Nigeria, interesting findings emerged – there was evidence of positive changes among supported women in community influencing, participation in community groups, and attitudes towards the rights of women in wider society. Where no evidence of change was detected, it tended to be in those indicators linked to issues at a more personal or household level, such as women's involvement in household decision-making and attitudes towards gender roles in the household.

It was interesting that these findings in many ways mirrored those from the first year of reviews, but the finer grain of the analysis permitted a more detailed picture of the state of empowerment. Sometimes, this revealed seemingly confusing or contradictory findings – for example, we found high levels of self-confidence among supported women, but very 'traditional' views on the role of women and men in the household, together with seemingly limited opportunities to participate in decision-making. This prompted a more detailed and enlightening discussion with the project team, aiming to understand more accurately the 'context of empowerment' in which the project was operating.

It also, in turn, prompted further deliberation on how to refine evaluation tools in order to make them more context-appropriate and sensitive to a wider range of aspects pertaining to empowerment. As a result of this, the framework employed in the latter part of 2012/13 and in the current round of reviews (2013/14) has been expanded and amended to cover five dimensions, and a greater number of constituent characteristics. The current framework offers a 'suite' of characteristics from which the evaluator and project team can then select those most appropriate to the project's theory of change and the particular context in question. So far, in practice, this has usually involved a review of the characteristics with the project team, and then some modest changes to the questionnaire depending on the context or specific focus of the project. These discussions have also sometimes revealed new characteristics which were previously omitted, and these can then be added to the 'menu' for future evaluations. It is hoped that by strengthening and embedding this approach in this iterative way the evaluation will be more appropriately tailored to the project's theory of change, and therefore both more valid and more useful for project, project team, and organisational learning (Table 4.2).

Critique

After three years of piloting and of regular and incremental improvements to the Effectiveness Reviews, it is both necessary and appropriate to step back and ask some bigger questions about the measurement approach that Oxfam GB has developed for the Women's Empowerment Effectiveness Reviews. Rather than provide a more detailed commentary on the more technical elements of the measurement approach, or broader challenges associated with the design and implementation of the organisational performance framework, we will focus in

Table 4.2 Suite of economic empowerment characteristics – years two and three

Dimension	Characteristics
Ability to make decisions and influence	Involvement in household investment decisions Involvement in livelihood management decisions Involvement in income-spending decisions Involvement in general decisions Degree of influence in community decision-making
Self-perception	Opinions on women's property rights Opinions on women's political rights Opinions on women's educational equality Opinions on women's economic and political roles Opinions on early marriage Self-confidence Psycho-social well-being
Personal freedom	Literacy Autonomy in work Time to pursue personal goals Support from family in pursuing personal goals Attitude to violence against women Experience of violence
Access to and control over resources	Ownership of land and property Ownership of other productive assets Independent income Extent of role in managing/keeping family's cash Savings Access to credit
Support from social networks	Degree of social connectivity Participation in community groups Level of support provided by groups to pursue own initiatives

this section on areas we see as most related to monitoring, evaluation, and learning (MEL) in the area of women's empowerment programming. Here, we draw out what we see as key areas for nuanced reflection and improvement, and set out a few challenges and areas for improvement in Oxfam's practice in coming years. We hope, of course, that these insights into Oxfam practice have interest and relevance for colleagues in other organisations developing their own methods for evaluating women's empowerment.

Whose empowerment?

As noted earlier, Oxfam GB's approach to organisational impact assessment was developed by a central evaluation team, at the request of senior leadership. The dimensions of empowerment outlined in the tool are the product of reviews of existing research, combined with inputs from Oxfam GB's gender advisers. During evaluation and survey design, data collection and analysis, evaluators must make a series of judgements that impact on how empowerment is defined and reported. For example, the construction of composite indices requires various value judgements at multiple stages of the aggregation process, including when assigning weights to the different dimensions under consideration, making composite indices necessarily subject to debate. While evaluators draw on experience and regularly seek out objective measures or advice from others, individual judgement is often required. In addition, the global effectiveness review team was initially comprised of men (though since 2013, both men and women) from fairly homogeneous backgrounds – they are all English-speaking, living in Oxford, from OECD countries, and university educated. This will inevitably lead to limitations and challenges in defining empowerment for people whose identities and realities are very different.

That said, pursuing this evaluation approach has provided the opportunity to have much more meaningful discussion with project teams, thematic leads, and senior management about what they actually mean by empowerment. This in itself represents organisational capacity building in the wider process of mainstreaming gender issues into Oxfam. In particular, project delivery teams have found that having a tangible evaluation framework as a starting point has allowed us to move beyond abstract concepts, and to pin down ideas into terms that make sense to project staff. During the evaluation design stage, the evaluator discusses with the project team how the project has been trying to affect changes in empowerment through the various project interventions. This exercise alone has generated valuable discussions and learning moments regarding assumptions around the rationale for the selected project interventions, and the 'theory of change', as well as the barriers and opportunities to empowerment in the particular context in which the project operates.

Referring again to the example from Nigeria, women supported by the project scored highly on the self-efficacy scale, which we, as outsiders, would normally assume to be an indicator of greater empowerment. At the same time these same women held what we might see as very 'traditional' views of the roles and responsibilities of men and women in the household – something which the Oxfam team determined (pre-analysis) were a marker of disempowerment.

While these two measures of empowerment are not necessarily mutually exclusive, reviewing the data and reflecting on our categorisation of 'traditional attitudes' generated debates within the evaluation team about what empowerment means to them.[8] It also prompted greater caution in determining how we score these different measures, and the danger of drawing too heavily on stereotyped or externally determined visions of empowerment. It also has to be acknowledged that by aggregating rich data into one composite index, one risks losing crucial information that might otherwise be useful to programme teams. In order to respond to this, we decided, in the most recent reviews, to give greater focus to the results on the individual indicators, enabling people with much greater understanding of women's empowerment in that context to explore the findings further.

Ensuring appropriate measurement

Beyond conceptual challenges, evaluation practitioners have a secondary task to contend with: finding appropriate tools to measure empowerment across the diversity of interventions that development organisations implement, while being sensitive to the diversity of context both across and within different countries and of identities and personalities among different women.

The evaluation team in Oxfam GB has attempted to address this issue by offering a suite (or 'menu') of indicators from which the project team and evaluator can select and use, depending on the aspects of empowerment that are seen to be most important and appropriate to the context and the changes the project is trying to effect.

Ensuring evaluation is guided by local definitions and understanding of empowerment is an improvement, but it is not enough. Decisions on what empowerment looks like for particular women in particular communities are still largely taken by people *working on* – and not necessarily participating in or being affected by – a project. We recognise that people affected by a project must be involved in determining its success (this is a given in Oxfam's approach to MEL, but is particularly critical in an empowerment project) – and the failure to do this meaningfully so far is one of the biggest shortfalls of the implementation of this approach to date.

We are, therefore, expecting to trial approaches that incorporate participatory methods at the beginning and end of the evaluation process – whereby, at a minimum, the decisions on which indicators are relevant for 'empowerment' among women living in a particular context are made (or at least informed) by those women themselves. How we do this is still to be determined, but different approaches could include better linking with a project's existing monitoring and accountability practices, incorporation of more 'immersive' research, or use of participatory processes at the evaluation design and the results interpretation stages. Regardless, simply bringing project participants into the discussion on what empowerment means or 'looks like' to them, in that particular context, is a critical next step. In the Nigerian example, doing so would have helped us make sounder judgements on what constitutes 'more' or 'less' empowered, as well as to interpret confusing or seemingly paradoxical results. We also anticipate involving local women will both help reveal new aspects of empowerment which otherwise may have been overlooked, and in itself be part of the empowerment process.

Valuing the right things

As a complex, somewhat intangible and multi-dimensional construct, women's empowerment involves many small and inter-dependent changes. However, it may be unrealistic to expect to detect changes in many of the indicators that are being measured over what is typically a short-term project lifespan (e.g. two to five years). Some empowerment indicators currently included in the framework, which probably feature in many log-frames connected to empowerment interventions, may be too 'ambitious' and the measurement tools used to assess them insufficiently sensitive to detect small changes or to take into account human complexity and power relationships. In the context of low-budget evaluations, this concern is aggravated by the fact that one needs a sufficiently large data set for small changes to be picked up as being statistically significant. If evaluation and measurement approaches are better able to discern and highlight smaller 'baby-steps' being achieved along the path to these longer-term outcomes, it would strengthen our analysis and understanding of contributing factors to empowerment. We are inspired by one example of hard-to-detect but meaningful steps, which many analytical approaches would bypass in search of 'higher returns'. One woman in a three-year empowerment project, quoted in Batliwala and Pittman (2010, 19) states:

> *Three years ago, when the landlord in whose fields I work addressed me, I would answer him looking down at his feet. Now, I answer with my eyes on his chest. Next year, I will be strong enough to look him right in the eyes when I speak to him.*

Taking the time to identify and then capture such nuances is essential, but the implications for cost and staff time may make this prohibitive to implement across all of our reviews. At a minimum, Oxfam staff and partners are challenged to trial different approaches to meaningful participation in a number of reviews, even as we make more modest improvements across the board.

Another challenge for this evaluation approach is to identity and assess 'unintended' or unexpected effects of programme activities. This is a standard limitation of fixed evaluation structures (that is, methods which are developed to evaluate success or otherwise in achieving pre-determined project outcomes) which has come into focus as the evaluation team looks at the evaluation's ability to understand how women's economic empowerment projects have affected care work.

Research has illuminated the ongoing imbalance in care work provided by women and Oxfam's own research has lately focused on how development interventions can worsen women's unequal load (Kidder 2013). This is one aspect that is clearly important to try to assess, but which is often neglected in evaluations of livelihoods and economic empowerment interventions. Projects often seek to increase women's empowerment in large part by providing economic opportunities specifically for women. In many of the contexts in which Oxfam implements these interventions, women are the main care providers – whether to children, elderly family members, or the household generally – and it is important to also consider the project's impact on women's time and energy and whether there has been any change in the division of labour in the household as a result. While changes in income and decision-making are being measured, the effect that interventions have in *adding to* women's existing roles and responsibilities is not sufficiently understood or measured. Economic interventions of the type described – whether aimed at a collective or more individual incomegenerating activity – have related and generally quite intensive demands on the participant's time and energy. It is fair to say that our evaluative work to date has not adequately assessed the knock-on effects of these demands on supported women's time or responsibilities.

Evaluation as a tool for empowerment and accountability

Demand for these evaluations was driven primarily by needs for organisational performance information, delivered through the application of rigorous and defensible evaluation methods. It is argued that such information would also lead to improvements in programme quality, at the project and perhaps at the organisational level. These evaluations have earned the recognition of external oversight bodies, such as the Department for International Development and 3ie, and from 2012/13 there has been an increasing focus on working with teams to build understanding and ownership of the questions the review are trying to answer and a commitment to undertake more follow-up research, to ensure that the findings are acted upon and influence practice. This is particularly impressive, considering budgetary constraints.

While credible performance information is now available to managers and funders (so-called 'upwards accountability'), the evaluation method has arguably involved trade-offs on accountability to partner organisations, as well as 'downwards', to communities and poor people. One could argue that ultimately Oxfam's primary stakeholders will benefit if the reviews are credible, and lead to Oxfam doing more of the things that are working and less of the things that are not, but the counter-argument is that the statistical methods employed by the evaluations are sometimes highly technical, and the purpose and results of the review are often not disseminated clearly to the communities involved. As an organisation committed to partnership, results, and 'downwards accountability', these reviews could provide Oxfam the opportunity through appropriate communication of results, and approaches such as empowerment evaluation, the means to both assess and promote women's empowerment.

The act of balancing accountability and learning demands is not new, and yet one in which there is continuing difficulty – getting the balance right is neither simple nor easy. Done poorly, evaluation approaches such as the one described in this paper can be tremendously *dis*empowering to field staff and, potentially, to beneficiary groups who become subjects in our scientific inquiry. It is clear that evaluators have an obligation to 'do no harm' through the application of their methods, and we would include in this a responsibility to guard against 'disempowering' ways of working.

The effectiveness review team have tried to do so in a number of ways, primarily through how technical specialists interact and work with partner and field staff. Detailed discussions explain the intent and method behind the evaluation; the survey is designed in conjunction with the local team; plainly written summaries explain technical results, and collaborative debriefing sessions help evaluators and field teams understand what the data are telling us about effectiveness. Oxfam also encourages the local team to share the results of the review with the project participants. In one case in Honduras, the results were also shared by the partner organisation with both intervention and comparison communities, which actively wanted to learn from the experiences of how the project had worked in their neighbouring communities. Country project teams have final comment on the evaluation report, through management responses which are published simultaneously with evaluation reports, on public websites.

One important note is that this approach was designed with the assumption that it would complement existing participatory programme monitoring and management processes. In reality, scarce resources, tight project timelines or under-involvement in monitoring and evaluation at the project design or review stages mean that detailed discussions about issues such as the 'dimensions of empowerment' may be missed. This approach could be strengthened to make the process more empowering for the people we work with, by incorporating the tool into a much earlier stage of the project cycle.

As with resilience, the process of developing, testing, and refining the measurement approach for empowerment is supporting Oxfam to be clearer about what empowerment means in a particular context, and arguably this could helpfully be used throughout the programme learning cycle – as a lens for analysis and scoping, to inform programme strategy/design, and develop appropriate monitoring and evaluation strategies. As mentioned above, one of the key benefits to date has been the starting point that the approach has provided in 'pinning down' what empowerment actually looks like or means for the team working on the project. If the discussions could be widened – as previously suggested – to women and men actually living in the project communities, and carried out through the whole life-cycle of the project, our feeling is that this would yield a much more informative and empowering process all round.

Conclusion

The goal of this paper has been to present and reflect critically on an evolving approach to assessing women's empowerment interventions. After three years of implementation, Oxfam's self-described 'experiment' in measuring organisational effectiveness has yielded not only huge amounts of survey data but also considerable lessons about both measurement approaches and our understanding of 'empowerment'. The challenge, of course, lies in translating those lessons into improved practice, so that evaluation exercises directly benefit those Oxfam works with in future.

This chapter has also examined a number of limitations and potential shortfalls in the current approach, asking questions about the definition of empowerment used and who should be involved in making decisions at different stages of the evaluation. We note some of the practical challenges encountered by the effectiveness review team over the last three years, as well as highlighting areas where the approach has evolved over time. It is our hope that such critical reflection will enable others to better understand and build on Oxfam's recent experience. Just as important, this has been an opportunity to document and share some of the tensions and trade-offs involved in the current approach. It will be a considerable (but potentially inspiring) challenge to Oxfam to further improve its current technically rigorous, pragmatically delivered approach in evaluations to come.

Acknowledgements

Thank you to Ines Smyth, Jennie Richmond, Rob Fuller, Bet Caeyers, and Claire Hutchings for their detailed, insightful, and challenging contributions to earlier versions of this paper.

Notes

1. As an organisation, Oxfam is committed to 'putting women's rights at the heart of all we do'. This is articulated as part of the organisation's 2013–2019 Strategic Plan, and has been a consistent instruction to staff at Oxfam GB for some time.
2. Oxfam is an international confederation of 17 organisations working together in more than 90 countries. Oxfam Great Britain (GB) is a member of Oxfam International. The Global Performance Framework and Project Effectiveness Reviews are initiatives of Oxfam GB, managed by Oxfam GB staff. This chapter usually uses the simpler term Oxfam, except when specificity is needed to help illustrate formal management and accountability lines.
3. It is important to note that the demand was for data that could be aggregated – but not compared. The evaluation framework does not allow for performance comparisons between very different projects and contexts.
4. From a quote attributed to Sheela Patel, Director of SPARC, India, in Batliwala and Pittman (2010, 7).
5. The authors wish to acknowledge the work of Claire Hutchings, Rob Fuller, Karl Hughes, and Bet Caeyers (effectiveness review team members) along with countless others who have contributed to improving this tool over time.
6. Each evaluation report includes detailed technical explanations of how this analysis is conducted. For example, we recommend reading pages 5–8 of the 2012 Nigerian project evaluation report (Oxfam GB 2012). For those new to these concepts, we recommend the 'Better Evaluation' website (www.betterevaluation.org) as a useful place to find accessible and clear background on evaluation methods.
7. We acknowledge that the idea of aggregating binary indicators to create an overall index of empowerment is not unique to OPHI. However,

OPHI's approach and thought leadership has had a large influence on Oxfam's approach to impact evaluation of 'large n' programmes.

8. There may also be some form of measurement error at play. Measures of some characteristics include self-reports on attitudes (e.g.'how much do you agree or disagree with this statement?'), and project participants may simply answer in ways that they think will please Oxfam. One might also suggest that women's attitudes about gender roles result from internalising social norms about women's subordinate role. Among this group of respondents, scores for 'self-efficacy', constructed from ten separate questions, were remarkably high. In this particular project at least, respondents appeared to be very strong and self-confident women with traditional beliefs about gender roles.

References

Alkire, Sabina, Ruth Meinzen-Dick, Amber Peterman, Agnes R. Quisumbing, Greg Seymour and Ana Vaz (2012) 'The Women's Empowerment in Agriculture Index: Discussion Paper', IFPRI, http://www.ifpri.org/publication/women-s-empowerment-agriculture-index (last checked by the authors December 2013).

Batliwala, Srilatha and Alexandra Pittman (2010) 'Capturing Change in Women's Realities: A Critical Overview of Current Monitoring and Evaluation Frameworks and Approaches', AWID, http://www.awid.org/About-AWID/AWID-News/Capturing-Change-in-Women-s-Realities (last checked by the authors May 2014).

Hughes, Karl and Claire Hutchings (2011) 'Can We Obtain the Required Rigor without Randomisation?', 3ie Working Paper No. 13, http://www.3ieimpact.org/en/evaluation/working-papers/working-paper-13/ (last checked by the authors May 2014).

Kabeer, Naila (1999) 'The Conditions and Consequences of Choice: Reflections on the Measurement of Women's Empowerment', United Nations Research Institute for Social Development (UNRISD) Discussion Paper No. 108, http://www.unrisd.org/unrisd/website/document.nsf/ab82a6805797760f80256b4f005da1ab/31eef181bec398a380256b67005b720a/$FILE/dp108.pdf (last checked by the authors December 2013).

Kidder, Thalia (2013) 'Care Work Discussions Happening in Rural Communities?! What Next?', http://policy-practice.oxfam.org.uk/blog/2013/10/care-work-discussions-in-rural-communities (last checked by the authors May 2014).

Oxfam GB (2012) 'Improving Women's Leadership and Effectiveness in Agricultural Governance [in Nigeria]: Project Effectiveness Review', Full evaluation technical report, http://policy-practice.oxfam.org.uk/publications/effectiveness-review-improving-womens-leadership-and-effectiveness-in-agricultu-303455 (last checked by the authors May 2014).

Oxford Poverty and Human Development Initiative (2014) 'Policy – A Multidimensional Approach', http://www.ophi.org.uk/policy/multidimensional-poverty-index/ (last checked by the authors May 2014).

About the authors

David Bishop is an independent evaluation consultant, currently working with Jenga Community Development Outreach in Uganda. From 2010 to 2013, he was part of the team who designed and delivered Oxfam's Global Performance Framework and led improvements in Oxfam's approach to measuring the effectiveness of women's economic empowerment programming. Postal address: JENGA CDO, PO Box 993, Mbale, Uganda. Email: dpbishop01@ hotmail.com.

Kimberly Bowman is a Global Adviser – Gender and MEL at Oxfam. Since 2013, she has supported MEL of women's economic empowerment programmes in Asia and looks forward to working with others to tackle some of the challenges outlined in this chapter. Postal address: Oxfam House, John Smith Drive, Oxford OX4 2JY, UK. Email: kbowman@oxfam.org.uk.

CHAPTER 5

Reflections on Womankind Worldwide's experiences of tackling common challenges in monitoring and evaluating women's rights programming

Helen Lindley

Abstract

There are a number of technical, conceptual, and institutional challenges in monitoring and evaluating programme work and advocacy on women's rights. Measuring progress and change is difficult because of the complexity and variety of the work involved in women's rights projects and programmes, and their limited time-frames. In order to capture change, to promote learning within development organisations and the broader sector, and secure donor investment and policymaker commitment to women's rights, it is vital to find creative ways to tackle these challenges. This chapter presents Womankind Worldwide's and partners' experiences in attempting to tackle some of these challenges by using Outcome Mapping-based approaches, in activities aiming to end violence against women and girls and promote women's participation.

Keywords: M&E, women's rights, Outcome Mapping, learning, violence against women and girls, participation

Introduction

Identifying and communicating change brought about by international development programming, advocacy, and campaigning is vital. Evidence of change is needed to strengthen learning within the sector, so that projects are relevant and effective for participants; it is also required to secure further donor investment and policymaker commitment to women's rights work. Sometimes, these objectives of both upwards and downwards accountability and learning are particularly hard to reconcile. A particular challenge is the relatively short time-span of development projects which are complex and varied, and aiming to have an impact on relationships and dynamics which are likely to take much longer to show real change.

Womankind Worldwide is an international women's rights organisation working to help women transform their lives in Africa, Asia, and Latin America.

http://dx.doi.org/10.3362/9781780447049.005

In addition to its own policy and advocacy work, Womankind currently works in solidarity with 35 partner women's rights organisations in 14 countries to implement programmes and conduct advocacy under the strategic objectives of women's participation, violence against women and girls (VAWG), and women's economic empowerment.

The nature, size, and objectives of Woman kind partners varies from national coalitions to smaller rural-based organisations, all of which play a key role in strengthening the women's movement in their countries and internationally. Womankind works directly with partners to implement programmes, and also supports its partners through a process involving joint identification of needs, and intensive accompaniment from Womankind Programme Managers, with targeted training and capacity building where needed. It seeks to support partners to strengthen and diversify their funding base, and manage the requirement and expectations of different donors. Womankind does not have any in-country presence itself, to avoid competing with partner organisations for sources of funding.

Womankind has an operational budget of £4.7 million and a presence in 14 countries. Womankind has a variety of funding sources, each with distinct monitoring and evaluation (M&E) and reporting needs; 70 per cent of funding is derived from statutory and institutional grants, such as UKaid and Comic Relief, and the remainder comes from individual giving, trusts, and legacies (Annual Report, 2012–3).

Currently, Womankind – in common with many other international development organisations – is increasing its investment in tools, approaches and systems to monitor and evaluate changes brought about by its work. Monitoring and evaluating development work intended to support women's ability to realise their rights involves specific technical and institutional challenges in identifying, measuring, communicating and understanding change.

This chapter presents and analyses key technical and institutional challenges that women's rights organisations and programmes commonly face in designing and implementing M&E approaches and systems. It then discusses Womankind and its partners' experience of tackling some of these challenges in their M&E of programmatic and advocacy work to end VAWG, and promote women's participation in decision-making. The chapter ends with a discussion of some practical lessons from our experience, and recommendations for both practitioners and policymakers. The examples from programme experience come from a series of M&E support visits to partner organisations conducted by the Womankind Monitoring, Evaluation and Learning Advisor and Programmes Team between October 2012 and November 2013.

The context: M&E challenges facing Womankind

Womankind and its partners are familiar with the need to have strong M&E systems. Over the years, both Womankind and partner staff have monitored the progress of programmes and advocacy, and sought to understand their

effectiveness and the changes in women's lives, through simple surveys, qualitative tools such as focus groups and in-depth interviews, staff's own observations, and the commissioning of external evaluations where appropriate.

The reality in which international development organisations work is complex at the best of times. In seeking to use resources to make the maximum
possible positive impact upon the lives of those we work with, learning about
both the effectiveness of individual programmes and of wider models and
approaches is a key aim of M&E in order to inform our current and future
work so that it builds upon this knowledge and learning.

Recognising these needs and challenges, Womankind undertook a Learning
Review in 2008 (Wallace and Fernandes Schmidt 2008) to understand better
the changes Womankind and partners were supporting, and Womankind's
positioning within the sector, and has increasingly invested in facilitating
mutual learning opportunities with partners.

M&E is also used for accountability purposes. International development
organisations work across multiple contexts, and they are answerable to multiple donors, including governmental and international agencies, trusts and
foundations funded by corporations or wealthy individuals, and private donors.

In recent years, a number of government and international agencies have
shifted towards Results-based Management approaches. Although donors
may have different systems, common to this approach is the definition of
clear results which are used to judge the success of a programme through the
measurement of progress against specific indicators.[1] In addition to reporting
results to specific donors, in 2010. Womankind was awarded a Programme
Partnership Agreement (PPA) with the UK government's Department for
International Development (DFID), providing unrestricted funding to
Womankind. This has necessitated the systematic reporting of results across
all Womankind programmes.

The demands for information for both learning and accountability have led to
us recognising the need to consider what kind of M&E systems and approaches
would enhance Womankind's ability to track and measure change systematically. The approach needs to be practical and realistic; sufficiently flexible to be
used in programmes of different sizes; and useful to our different partner organisations, which have different capacities to absorb new M&E tools and ways of
working. Finally, any approach taken needs to reflect Womankind's partnership
values. These are to work in co-ordination with partners, to build upon partner
systems in place, to engage partners in the design and development of monitoring, evaluation, and learning frameworks and tools; and to strengthen not only
Womankind's own reporting, but partners' own M&E systems.

M&E of women's rights – technical and institutional challenges

The increased focus on demonstrating and understanding change is both necessary and welcome. However, it throws up particular challenges to organisations working on women's rights. They may be development organisations

which focus on women's rights as one element of many, or specialist women's rights organisations. They may be large organisations working internationally, or local organisations focusing on the specific interests of women in one particular country. All of these are finding they are needing to invest in M&E, focus on this in innovative and creative ways, and engage in dialogue with others to exchange ideas.[2]

Defining changes associated with women's rights and empowerment

Many of the changes that these interventions seek to bring about may be hard to conceptualise and define in measurement terms. Whereas a development intervention seeking to increase access to clean water, for example, can decide on indicators which focus on tangible, material changes, many of the changes we are interested in (subjective) understandings of abstract ideas. This highlights the power dynamics involved in who decides how changes such as 'women's empowerment' are defined, and subsequently what is measured.

For example, the aim of 'women's empowerment' is a constructed concept which contains multiple components, such as self-confidence and control over decision-making, which are subject to multiple interpretations (Kabeer 1998). These concepts are not only understood differently by many different researchers, practitioners, and policymakers, depending on their politics and their understanding of development and women's rights and the connections between the two; they are also influenced by and defined by individual experience, position, and location. Gender, race, socio-economic background, and other aspects of identity define everyone's views about empowerment and what it looks like. In practical terms, this creates challenges in developing appropriate measures of such changes.

Observing change to gender power relations: sensitivities around this

Even when clearly defined, some changes may be technically difficult and sensitive to observe, such as changes in social norms surrounding the acceptability of violence or in household power dynamics. Promising best practice has been developed in the use or, for example, survey questions to measure reductions in violence (World Health Organisation, London School of Hygiene and Tropical Medicine, South African Medical Research Council 2013) or changes in social norms (Mackie *et al.* 2012). In addition to technical challenges such as social desirability bias,[3] however, integrating such techniques into routine M&E, where the technical capacity of teams may be lower, is a long-term process.

A second issue which is important in M&E of women's rights interventions – in particular those operating at the grassroots community level – is the identity of the observer, which is imbued with power and needs to be taken into account. The power the observer holds (which is related to his or her gender identity as well as to other aspects including race and class) is important because this may skew or affect results. For example, if an evaluator sits in a women's group meeting to observe the meeting, this may well affect the behaviour of the participants and the issues discussed.

Quality versus quantity? Measuring, comparing, and aggregating change

Many women's rights programmes and organisations have attempted to tackle these challenges through the use of qualitative methods, and have unearthed valuable results. Qualitative research methods, however, have historically encountered pre-judices in the social sciences (and in practice and policy relating to social change) as they are perceived to be less 'scientific' than quantitative methods. In line with Results-based Management approaches, both donors and Programme Managers require quantified results which can be summarised to track the progress of a project or multiple projects over time, and compared with other projects in different contexts.

Whilst some changes programmes may seek to achieve, such as an increase in the number of women Members of Parliament (MPs), lend themselves to quantification and aggregation, there is the risk that success is defined according to those changes that can be easily quantified as opposed to changes which are more suited towards qualitative data collection. For example, as one woman politician supported by Womankind partner Zambia National Women's Lobby described, the nature of women's participation in politics, and the experiences they face, can be as important to measure as simply the number of women in Parliament:

> Women candidates are given a lot of names and called prostitutes in campaigns. Men used to intimidate women before I knew the Women's Lobby. (Focus Group conducted as part of external evaluation, Solwezi Women Politicians, Zambia; Womankind 2014a)

A risk is that if success is increasingly defined by quantitative indicators, then meaningful signs of change which are harder to quantify, such as an increase in the self-confidence of a survivor of violence, are not valued, making some projects less attractive to donors. Tackling this challenge requires both creative ways of expressing and summarising qualitative change, and a recognition of the value of measuring changes more suited towards qualitative data collection.

Capturing and analysing long-term change

Changing gender relations, and attitudes and beliefs about gender issues and women's rights, is a long-term process, yet it is rare that international development programmes continue longer than three to five years. When identifying changes to measure as part of project frameworks, the length of time real shifts will take to come about needs to be considered, and appropriate indicators chosen. For example, although a 'reduction in violence against women' may be the key change a prevention programme seeks to achieve, this is rarely feasible or realistic in a typical project time-frame of a few years.

When defining changes to measure it is therefore important to consider what changes might be expected to be seen, in whom, and at what point in time, in order to develop 'signposts' of change, placing emphasis on short- to medium-term changes which may often be overlooked. These changes should be closely linked to how it is envisaged a programme will influence change. For example, projects which seek to raise women's knowledge of the existence of local service providers for cases of violence, and support women's confidence and ability to access services if needed, may result in an increase in the number of women reporting cases of violence in the short term. Viewing these statistics without knowledge of the programme's theory, what changes it expected to achieve, and when, would risk painting a picture of failure.

Institutional challenges

The increased emphasis on M&E in Results-based Management poses particular issues for some kinds of work and types of organisation. Large international development organisations may be better able to find unrestricted funding to invest in M&E, but many partner organisations (including small development non-government organisations (NGOs) and also women's rights organisations) not only have lower technical M&E experience and capacity, but often have challenges in funding their core organisational costs (Esplen 2013), and investing in strengthening their institutions. Even if funding for an M&E Officer may be partly or fully in place, and the institutional will exists to strengthen an organisation's M&E, if an organisation is struggling to pay the salaries of other staff or does not have resources to travel to communities to monitor activities, then M&E is much less likely to move forward.

Womankind's approach to M&E of women's rights

Core principles underlying Womankind's M&E

In addressing these challenges, Womankind has taken a three-pronged approach in its M&E:

1. Engagement with partners to define and unpack the changes they wish to achieve.
2. The use of these definitions of change to develop frameworks and specific tools which can be used to collect, analyse, and understand changes.
3. The collation and aggregation, where needed, of change across programmes.

To support this, Womankind combined the principles of feminist evaluation, the practical use of Outcome Mapping and Outcome Harvesting, and used a range of data collection tools.

Rather than providing a specific framework or an approach, *feminist evaluation* entails a set of values and ways of working that place emphasis upon understanding women's experiences and viewpoints, whilst recognising that the analysis and interpretation of these are mediated by the socioeconomic, cultural, and political background of the evaluator (Podems 2010).

Outcome Mapping is an approach which supports the identification and measurement of specific behavioural changes in 'Boundary Partners' – that is, those actors within an organisation's sphere of influence[4]. Through a process in which an organisation defines the changes in behaviour, relationships, actions, and activities that it would expect to, like to, and love to see in each Boundary Partner (whether an individual or a group), the approach shifts the emphasis of monitoring to assessing progress against these changes, and understanding the organisation's contribution to change (Earl *et al.* 2001).

Outcome Harvesting is a method which, rather than measuring progress against pre-established outcomes as you may find in a log-frame, supports the identification and collation of positive and negative, intentional and unintentional changes as they emerge. 'Outcomes' are defined as specific observable changes in the behaviour of an individual, group, organisation, or institution (Wilson-Grau and Britt 2012). When used in monitoring, outcomes can be identified and collated on an ongoing basis through observations or additional monitoring tools. When used in an evaluation, outcomes are identified and collated retrospectively.

Womankind has adapted the methodology of Outcome Mapping, originally developed by the International Development Research Centre in 2001, to establish a means with which to engage partners in clearly identifying the changes it sought to achieve and explore the thinking behind these, as a basis for collecting data on these changes. This process sought to move M&E away from seeking programme outcomes phrased in relation to 'improved policies and practices' or 'improved attitudes' to define specific changes that could be observed and monitored.

The Womankind four-step process

The process comprises four steps:

1. Identifying the stakeholders that a partner will engage with and seeks to influence.
2. Identifying 'Progress Markers'. Rather than quantitative indicators, these are descriptive statements which refer to a series of changes that the programmes expect, would like to, and would love to achieve, particularly small changes, which are often overlooked but which also may be the first signs of progress in a programme. In reference to a metaphor of a winding road, these changes are 'signposts' that let you know if you are going in the right direction.

3. Identifying how and when changes relating to these Progress Markers could be observed during the programme – this might be through direct observation of a meeting, a conversation in a community, or the use of a tool such as a focus group. Data collection could include both quantitative and qualitative methods.
4. Analysing and reporting progress against Progress Markers – an analysis of progress against Progress Markers using both quantitative and qualitative information.

The method is initially facilitated by the Womankind Monitoring, Evaluation and Learning Advisor or Programme Manager with partner organisation staff, with the aim of enabling staff to be able to repeat the process themselves in the future.

By placing focus upon clearly unpacking and identifying the change, rather than the technical M&E tool being used, this process provides a strong basis which data collection can subsequently build upon. When facilitating this process with partner organisation staff, ranging from an organisation's Director, through Programme Manager, to staff working directly with community members, it is a means to engage staff in developing common understandings of specific changes they are seeking to achieve in a programme, highlighting areas where there may be disagreement, and beginning to unearth their assumptions and beliefs. These shared understandings and conscious debates are important not only to strengthen the implementation and M&E of a particular programme, but can begin to facilitate deeper discussion around how we think change happens.

Building frameworks and specific tools upon definitions of change

Once Progress Markers have been developed and agreed, they can subsequently be used as a basis for reporting frameworks and/or the development of specific tools. When used as reporting frameworks, they provide a means to collectively analyse the extent to which change in the Progress Markers is being observed using direct observation and qualitative data collection methods, such as guiding the development of focus group questions, or as a field journal to record observations from community meetings and fields, in a simple form (Table 5.1).

This approach works particularly well for programmes where there are direct observable changes that can be recorded during meetings, such as governance and accountability programmes. In Kenya and Ghana, for example, as part of an existing monitoring schedule, partner organisations had planned visits to facilitate and observe quarterly meetings between women MPs/District Leaders and female constituents. The meetings were a rich source of qualitative information concerning what actions the leaders had taken since the last meeting, to what extent the female constituents were able to plan and develop proposals to submit to the leaders, and to what extent the leaders

Table 5.1 Example Outcome journal

Stakeholder:		
Level of change	Progress Marker	Description of change
Low	'Signpost of change'	Who did or said what, when, where, why is this important?
Medium		
High		

were responding to complaints and demands, however, there was no means to record, analyse, and report systematically upon these changes.

Following the development of Progress Markers for the women leaders and constituents, staff subsequently used these as a framework for taking notes during the meetings according to the changes they were trying to observe. Following the meetings these notes were used as a basis for team discussion to complete the journals (Table 5.2).

In some cases, it can be more appropriate to use the Progress Markers as a basis for the development of specific monitoring tools, such as observation forms and community-based surveys. Whilst the Progress Markers provide a framework, it can sometimes be used to develop more structured checklists, for example when repeatedly measuring whether an individual stakeholder is changing clearly defined behaviour. In 2013, in Kenya, Womankind partner Centre for Rights, Education and Awareness (CREAW) used the exercise to define specific changes in the behaviour of Police Officers concerning the treatment of survivors of violence, as follows.

Table 5.2 Excerpt from an Outcome journal from Ghana

Progress Marker – District Assembly (DA) and Unit Committee Representatives:	*Description of change*
Attend Gender Centre meetings, particularly the decision-makers	Four members of the DA attended but not the District Coordinating Director (DCD).
Acknowledge the importance of involving constituents in decision-making/seeking their views	The DA members there acknowledged that they should hold meetings however several DA members also noted that community members don't attend meetings organised, or don't turn up on time.
Make formal commitments during meetings about what actions they will take	One DA member said that she will attend a meeting on Wednesday organised by the Market Women's Association in order to discuss issues of security. One DA member said they will support the Dressmakers Association in writing a proposal to win contracts to sew school uniforms.

Police Officers:

- Correctly complete PR3 forms (e.g. they put in the correct date).
- Receive women at the Gender Desk, not in the middle of the office.
- Do not use derogatory language.
- Read a woman's statement back to the woman for verification that it is accurate.

As CREAW staff were able to observe directly to what extent this behaviour was being displayed through observations of Case Managers when accompanying women to the Police Station, this list of behaviours was turned into a Service Provider Monitoring Form – a checklist for the Case Managers to complete after each visit, with space for comments.

In community-based programmes, such as those that seek to change attitudes and behaviour of individual men and women, although the journals can be a useful tool of triangulation, for example through observing a community meeting, the Progress Markers can also be used to provide a structured means of data collection through the development of surveys, which are often the most feasible means to structure data collection across a geographically wide and diverse area.

An example comes from Zambia, where Womankind used the development of Progress Markers as a facilitation exercise with its partner, Women for Change, in order to identify specific changes in individuals that could be used as survey questions for a survey of knowledge, attitudes, and practices.

In addition to using international best practice questions, however, such as from the Gender Equitable Men Scale (Pulerwitz and Barker 2008), Womankind worked with field-based facilitators to develop specific Progress Markers for what 'change would look like' in different individuals. This exercise provided a means to move beyond conceiving of change in terms of 'women are involved in household decision-making' to develop consensus on what this would look like, and how it would be observed, in this specific context. This helped bring out the facilitators' own knowledge, in which they identified that the key way of knowing who had influence over household resources would be to ask:

When a family member dies, who makes the decision on what happens to land and property?
Man
Woman
Both

This involvement in shaping the survey was particularly important, as the facilitators were to be responsible for administering the survey, analysing results, and feeding them into their future engagement in communities.

A number of Womankind-supported programmes also provide training and services such as legal aid, psychological and medical support, shelter, and income generation training to individual women who have experienced violence and discrimination. In such programmes, in attempting to understand the changes that individual women experience through this support and the extent they are able to maintain these changes, Womankind's experience has similarly been that more structured data collection tools can be built upon definitions of change developed with partners. In Ethiopia and Nepal, Womankind drew from the Outcome Mapping methodology to develop and test a process to engage with partners in defining the areas in which they sought to support change in individual women, and what the journey these women might be expected to take looked like. These descriptions of change were subsequently integrated into a visual 'star' tool which is used to structure longitudinal interviews with individual women during their time receiving support and afterwards. The tool has been called the 'Empowerment Star' in these two country programmes, to enable Womankind and partners to define and express what they understand is different areas of 'empowerment' important in the context of their work.

Each area of change, such as self-confidence and self-esteem, forms a point of the star, with the 'rungs' of the ladder under each point describing what a woman might think, feel and act like at each stage in her journey (Table 5.3).

Importantly, these descriptions of change are not prescriptive – the journey that each woman faces will be unique and is unlikely to be linear. However, there may be elements in common which can be used as a framework for the analysis of more in-depth qualitative information. The use of a scale as a guide means that the information collected can also be quantified and measured using an indicator if needed.

In Peru, in attempting to define and understand the changes groups of women community-based organisation members who had received training on leadership, advocacy, and rights had experienced, the women themselves were supported to define criteria for 'Empowerment' or 'what a powerful woman looks like', and score progress against these criteria. This methodology built upon work originally undertaken by the Chars Livelihood Programme

Table 5.3 Excerpt from Empowerment Star, Women for Human Rights, Nepal

Area of change: safety and freedom from violence

Stage of change	Description of change
1	She thinks that is still not safe at the safe house. She feels that she is the only one experiencing violence. She doesn't want to do anything, she won't accept help from others.
2	She will think that she is in the right place to receive help; 'I am facing violence and I can get help'. She will feel that she isn't the only one who has been violated, that there are other women like her, that she is more secure. She understands that there are people willing to help her and understand the feelings she is going through and the violence that she has faced.

in Bangladesh in developing an Empowerment Score-card (McIntosh 2012) and provided a means and space to allow women themselves opportunity to voice changes significant to them, in a way which could be quantified and reported upon. The importance of supporting the women directly involved with the project to define 'empowerment' was realised when the same exercise was repeated with the Project Staff, who clearly described how empowerment may vary according to a woman's background. For an indigenous woman it may be seen in terms of having access to land, water, and resources; for a richer Peruvian woman a sign of empowerment may be being able to influence decision-making; and for a rural woman it may be not being beaten very often, or denouncing the violence they face. The final criteria developed by women representatives of community-based organisations included some perhaps surprising components such as 'communicates, shares, teaches' and 'shares experience', which would have been harder to predict (Womankind 2014b).

Collating and aggregating change

Whilst the adapted Outcome Mapping methodology and associated tool described above have contributed to the strengthening of partner programmatic M&E and understandings of change, Womankind was left with the challenge of collating the information collected across programmes. In addition, reporting for Womankind's DFID PPA required a means to aggregate changes as Outcome indicators.

Through the integration of the Outcome Mapping methodology into partner organisations' M&E, Womankind has begun to identify a series of different specific changes in the following classification of different actors that partners are directly trying to influence and benefit from the programme:

- Survivor of violence.
- Male community member(s).
- Female community member(s).
- Women's groups.
- Woman aspiring leader.
- MP (male/female).
- Local elected/nominated leader (male/female).
- Other policymaker.
- Service provider (e.g. Police).
- Traditional/community/religious leader.
- Media (including individual journalists).
- Project volunteers, e.g. paralegals.

Drawing from Outcome Harvesting, Womankind has created a form to collate and synthesise the changes being reported in different actors through journals, M&E tools, and partner Annual Reports (Table 5.4).

For aggregation purposes, the number of specific evidenced reports of change in different actors can subsequently be recorded in a database and

Table 5.4 Example use of Outcome Harvesting form

Change	Of the 37 aspiring grassroots women candidates identified and trained by Malawi National Women's Lobby [MNWL] in 2009, 34 candidates are now preparing to stand in 2013 Local Government Elections.
Significance	It is firstly significant that such a high proportion of those trained four years prior to the election date remain motivated and are ready to stand for election. Secondly, the women's background is particularly significant – the women were identified from women's listener clubs, established by the MNWL in their communities, and 32 of the women reported never previously having spoken in public in their communities before (see FGD [focus group discussion] for details).
Partner contribution	MNWL established 80 Women's Radio Listen Clubs, comprised of 1342 members, as part of a five year (2008–13) Women's Leadership Project. As part of the listener club activities, aspiring women leaders were identified, and provided with leadership training, including on formal rules, processes, and leadership skills. In a FGD in Rumphi, Malawi in July 2013, the women aspiring leaders noted that the clubs provide a politically neutral environment where all the aspiring leaders can interact with each other, share ideas and experiences regardless of their political affiliation.
Classification	Type of change Actor Country Partner Funder
Evidence	*Description of evidence* *Insert evidence*

reported as indicators. The original Outcome Harvesting methodology defined Outcomes as specific changes in the behaviour of individuals, groups, or institutions. As changes in both knowledge and attitudes are central to the Theory of Change for many women's rights programmes, the decision was made to replace the word 'outcome' with 'change' and log changes in knowledge and attitude in addition to changes in behaviour.

Given the number and variety of Womankind partner programmes, and the varying start dates, this provides an overall 'snapshot' for global reporting purposes and a means of information management. The ACT Programme in Tanzania, however, managed by KPMG, has pioneered the aggregation of changes from Outcome journals for a specific governance programme and reporting to DFID, which provides more focused information (Dyer 2012).

Tracking incremental change

The approach has been particularly useful in firstly placing value upon, and providing a means to track, incremental change, in addition to singular changes at the outcome level. An example of a smaller incremental change that may be overlooked was identified by Womankind partner CREAW in Kenya, in the context of a programme which sought to strengthen the response of the Police Service to survivors of violence. In addition to identifying specific changes in the behaviour of the Police as Progress Markers, the partner identified a marker as follows:

The people from the correct Police Departments attend training sessions on VAWG. (Womankind Workshop with CREAW staff, Nairobi, 8 October 2013)

Partner staff regarded this change as signifying a shift in the value the Police Commissioner placed upon the training provided by the partner, through sending the appropriate staff, as requested. This is an example of a 'signpost' which indicates if a programme is progressing in the right direction, but which may not be captured with traditional indicators. In advocacy programmes, similarly, a commonly mentioned change is:

Policymaker attends meetings him/herself, as opposed to sending their assistant. (Womankind Workshop with CREAW staff, Nairobi, Kenya, 8 October 2013)

Secondly, the process of defining Progress Markers has in some cases supported partners to articulate and define, as a basis for measurement, the nuance of change. In Kenya again, in the context of a programme that aims to strengthen the accountability of women MPs and leaders to their female constituents, in addition to defining Progress Markers according to the number of complaints women MPs respond to, and the number and type of actions taken, CREAW staff identified as a Progress Marker:

Women leaders are articulating their challenges to constituents and explaining what they can't do and why. (Womankind Workshop with CREAW staff, Nairobi, 8 October 2013)

This change could be tracked through observation of quarterly meetings between the MPs and constituents, and was considered significant as it described a shift in the relationship between the two parties necessary in order to sustain change in the long term. Similarly, in Afghanistan, in the context of a programme which sought to strengthen the implementation of the Ending Violence Against Women Law (EVAW), instead of defining change in terms of the number of cases of VAWG that were successfully prosecuted, Womankind partners defined a key change as:

Articles of the Ending Violence Against Women Law are mentioned during cases, regardless of the outcome. (Womankind Workshop, Kabul, 17 September 2013)

Finally, the process, through defining changes that a programme is seeking to achieve, also provides a framework to capture and report clearly unanticipated changes that were not originally identified as Progress Markers. Womankind partner reports have revealed the importance of including space to allow partners to demonstrate influence of external actors and events in both revealing the extent of change, and driving change. In the context of a programme which aimed to change behaviour to women MPs, a partner explained how a revealing but unexpected change was when a political party they were trying to engage with did not sanction a male MP who publicly slapped a woman leader. In Kenya again, FIDA Kenya reported that publicity surrounding the anticipated enactment of the Family Bills had seen an increased number of women visiting their office to enquire about their rights under the bills and legal aid, despite the fact that the Bills had not yet been passed.

Conclusions: lessons and recommendations for NGOs and donors

The following lessons and recommendations are based upon Womankind's experiences to date for both practitioners and donors.

Invest time and actively engage in understanding the dynamics of change

Before the design of M&E tools and systems begins, it is important to invest time in identifying and understanding the dynamics under way in change with those partners or field staff who will be responsible for implementing the programme. Investing time in this process provides a strong basis from which M&E tools can be developed and findings analysed, but is an important step in revealing assumptions about how we think change happens.

Donors should encourage grantees to engage staff in this process in a practical way which is appropriate to their circumstances, whether it be through Outcome Mapping, Theories of Change, or 'light touch' methods, and build in grant start-up periods which help facilitate this. Where possible, this process should also include project participants, in order to explore how women and different actors see change as happening, and what is relevant and meaningful change to them. Following this process, there should be flexibility from donors in modifying the outcomes and indicators originally defined in a project proposal to reflect the reality of the programme.

Simple tools and creative reporting format that support nuanced identification and reporting of change

Build simple qualitative and quantitative tools upon these definitions and frameworks of change. Reporting formats provided by donors and the indicators programmes report upon should reflect the time-frame of the project, and the nuanced nature of the changes being measured. If using log-frame reporting formats, donors should include sections which encourage programmes to report upon intermediary change, and changes which are less easily quantified in a structured way, rather than leaving this just to the narrative section. Donors should recognise when aggregation is and is not possible, useful, and meaningful, and discuss with NGOs alternative ways to ensure accountability, capture progress, and report against change.

Understand institutional resources available and constraints

Both NGOs and donors should recognise that although creativity in approaches to tackle technical M&E challenges is important, this can be considerably facilitated or constrained by institutional resources and culture. Both donors and NGOs working with partners, particularly women's rights organisations, need to take a holistic approach when examining M&E capacity, which analyses not only if an M&E Officer, tools, and systems are in place, but how the strengths and structures of all levels of an organisation can support and constrain M&E. This extends from the extent to which field staff have sufficient time during visits to take and write up notes, to whether and if there are sufficient office staff to process, analyse, and learn from information.

The variety, complex nature, and difficulty of observing changes which women's rights programmes and advocacy seeks to achieve, and the limited time-frames in which to report progress on programmes that seek structural change, presents a number of technical, conceptuall and institutional challenges for programmes and organisations that work on women's rights. Womankind has begun to tackle these challenges through supporting partners in a process which places an emphasis on 'unpacking' these changes, and using mixed-methods tools which are appropriate to the context and resources available. This is a practical step that can be integrated into new and existing programmes. M&E, however, cannot take place in a vacuum, and needs to be supported by wider institutional support and investment to ensure that women's rights organisations have the institutional capacity to tackle these challenges. More fundamentally, however, these challenges raise questions for the sector and donors concerning what is feasible and appropriate in different circumstances, for different purposes.

Acknowledgements

Thank you to Womankind Programme staff Christiana Conte, Reineira Arguello, Cintia Lavandera, Catherine Klirodotakou, Wendy Ngoma, Susana Klein, and Tsitsi Matekaire, and partners AWSAD, CREAW, the Gender Centre, Women for Change, DEMUS, FIDA Kenya, Women for Human Rights, AWN, HAWCA, and the Malawi National Women's Lobby for their support and engagement in the M&E process described in this chapter.

Notes

1. Results-based Management is commonly characterised by the 'results chain' which outlines a programme's logic as follows:
   Inputs → Outputs → Outcomes → Impact.
   Each stage of the results chain is measured, and the actual results compared to the targets in order to judge performance. A clear critique of Results-based Management can be found at: http://www.mango.org.uk/Guide/WhyRBMnotWork (last checked by the author April 2014).

2. These challenges are common with other 'Hard to Measure Benefits'. This framework draws upon work carried out by DFID Programme Partnership Agreement Agencies through a Hard to Measure Learning Group, and discussed during an event at DFID in October 2013.
3. Social desirability bias refers to the tendency of respondents to respond to a question with the answer they think is socially acceptable or desirable. This is particularly true of sensitive subjects, such as violence against women and girls or social norms, where respondents may be aware that admitting personal attitudes, such as whether or not they think violence is acceptable under different circumstances, is not desirable. For more information, see http://bit.ly/1gVIamI (last checked by the author May 2014).
4. Although Outcome Mapping uses the language of 'Boundary Partners', Womankind refers to these individuals or groups as 'stakeholders', so as not to introduce additional M&E language.

References

Dyer, Kate (2012) 'Theory of change, outcome mapping and ACT'S logical framework', http://www.accountability.or.tz/wp-content/uploads/2013/03/Update-on-Think-Piece-Final.pdf (last checked by the author May 2014).

Earl, Sarah, Fred Carden, and Terry Smutylo (2001) 'Outcome mapping: building learning and reflection into development programs', http://www.outcomemapping.ca/resource/resource.php?id=269 (last checked by the author May 2014).

Esplen, Emily (2013) 'Leaders for change: why support women's rights organisations?', Womankind Worldwide, http://www.womankind.org.uk/wp-content/uploads/downloads/2013/03/LeadersForChange-FINAL.pdf (last checked by the author May 2014).

Kabeer, Naila (1998) *Money Can't Buy Me Love? Re-evaluating Gender, Credit and Empowerment in Rural Bangladesh*, IDS Discussion Paper 363, Brighton: Institute of Development Studies.

Mackie, Gerry, Francesca Moneti, Elaine Denny, and Holly Shakya (2012) *What Are Social Norms? How Are They Measured?* New York: UNICEF and San Diego: UCSD Center on Global Justice.

McIntosh, Ross (2012) 'Reviewing the CLP's approach to measuring women's empowerment', http://www.clp-bangladesh.org/pdf/monitoring%20women%5c's%20empowerment(3).pdf (last checked by the author May 2014).

Podems, Donna (2010) 'Feminist evaluation and gender approaches: there's a difference?', *Journal of MultiDisciplinary Evaluation* 6(14): 1–17.

Pulerwitz, Julie and Gary Barker (2008) 'Measuring attitudes toward gender norms among young men in Brazil: Development and psychometric evaluation of the GEM scale', *Men and Masculinities* 10(3): 322–338, http://www.popcouncil.org/research/measuring-attitudes-toward-gender-norms-among-young-men-in-brazil-developme (last checked by the author May 2014).

Wallace, Tina and Brita Fernandes Schmidt (2008) *A Journey Not a Destination – Womankind Worldwide Learning Review* (Internal document).

Wilson-Grau, Ricardo and Heather Britt (2012) 'Outcome Harvesting: The Ford Foundation's Middle East and North Africa Office' http://www.outcomemapping.ca/resource/resource.php?id=374 (last accessed by the author May 2014).

Womankind (2014a) *Womankind Learning and Evidence Review* (Internal document).

Womankind (2014b) *Snapshot of Change – Women's Empowerment in Peru* (Internal document).

World Health Organization, London School of Hygiene and Tropical Medicine, South African Medical Research Council (2013) *Global and Regional Estimates of Violence against Women: Prevalence and Health Effects of Intimate Partner Violence and Non-partner Sexual Violence*, Geneva: WHO.

About the author

Helen Lindley is the Monitoring, Evaluation and Learning Advisor at Womankind Worldwide. Before joining Womankind Helen worked on M&E on humanitarian and community-based rights, gender and health programmes in Senegal, Mali, and Haiti. Postal address: Womankind Worldwide, Development House, 56–64 Leonard Street, London EC2A 4LT, UK. Email: helen.lindley@gmail.com.

CHAPTER 6

Capturing changes in women's lives: the experiences of Oxfam Canada in applying feminist evaluation principles to monitoring and evaluation practice

Carol Miller and Laura Haylock

Abstract

Current trends in the aid environment pose significant challenges for effectively evaluating gender equality and women's rights programmes. This requires approaches that can capture and tell the complex story of how gender power relationships are challenged and changed. This chapter describes Oxfam Canada's efforts to develop a mixed-methods approach to monitoring, evaluation, and learning rooted in feminist evaluation principles, for Engendering Change, a multi-year, donor co-funded 'standalone' women's rights programme. The approach we developed was shaped by the external aid environment with its results orientation, as well as by our aspirations to bring feminist principles to our monitoring and evaluation practice. The chapter describes our understanding of feminist evaluation and what we believed it offered to strengthen our approach to monitoring and evaluation. Three examples of evaluative exercises used in the Engendering Change programme are provided to demonstrate how we attempted to bring the principles of feminist evaluation into practice.

Keywords: feminist evaluation, gender-sensitive evaluation, mixed-methods approaches to evaluation, gender power relations, transformative change, balancing learning and accountability

Introduction

Trends in the current aid environment, including the predominance of the logical framework approach and the emphasis on results that are relatively easy to measure, pose significant challenges for understanding and capturing how changes happen in women's lives. This point has been well-made by women's rights researchers and activists including Srilatha Batiliwala and Alexandra Pitman (2010). This chapter focuses on Oxfam Canada's efforts to respond to challenges we faced monitoring and evaluating a transformative women's rights programme by adopting a mixed-methods approach to

http://dx.doi.org/10.3362/9781780447049.006

evaluation rooted in feminist evaluation principles. Specifically, it explores what applying feminist principles to evaluation practice offers to organisations seeking to tell the complex story of how development programmes can contribute to lasting changes in gender power relations.

Examples shared in this chapter are drawn from Engendering Change (EC), a stand-alone women's rights and gender equality programme co-funded with the Canadian International Development Agency (CIDA), and implemented by Oxfam Canada between 2009 and 2014, with a total budget of $17.5 million. The EC programme included a portfolio of 44 partner organisations of different sizes, budgets, and missions, working in regions and countries as diverse as Central America and Cuba, the Horn and East Africa, southern Africa, and Asia. Partners included women's and feminist organisations and networks, as well as mixed non-government organisations (NGOs), membership organisations, and co-operatives. What brought these diverse organisations together in the EC programme was a shared commitment to working to support women to further gender equality and secure their rights. The EC programme provided partner organisations with organisational capacity building to support their path to becoming stronger, gender-just organisations (Oxfam Canada 2012a, 2012b). Organisational capacity-building support included, for example, gender mainstreaming support (Gonzalez Manchón and McLeod 2010) promoting transformative women's leadership, encouraging dialogue on gender issues, supporting gender budgeting, development of sexual harassment policies, and interventions to support work–life balance. At the same time, the EC programme provided partner organisations with a mix of core funding and specific funding for programme support in thematic areas such as women's leadership, women's economic empowerment, and elimination of gender-based violence. Programme support funding primarily funded project and activities that partner organisations themselves designed and implemented in response to community-identified needs and issues.

Some evaluation challenges

Like other feminist development practitioners, as monitoring, evaluation, accountability, learning (MEAL) staff we found ourselves facing multiple challenges when designing and implementing a monitoring and evaluation system that would help capture transformative change in a complex programme such as EC.[1] EC represented one of Oxfam Canada's first efforts to implement a large-scale 'programme', in the sense of a set of strategically aligned, mutually reinforcing interventions that contributes to sustained, positive impact on poor people's lives. This created an imperative to aggregate results and foster programme learning across the diverse set of partners and largely locally-designed and implemented projects.

Oxfam Canada has a long history of working in solidarity with, and accompanying, partner organisations. This history influenced the way in which monitoring and evaluation needed to be carried out in the organisation. Oxfam

Canada staff position themselves as co-learners working alongside partners in relationships of trust and mutual respect, to identify relevant issues and effective gender equality and women's rights strategies. These two interconnected challenges meant that, on the one hand, we needed to find some methods that would allow us to generate results that could be aggregated, compared, and contrasted. On the other, we needed to use monitoring and evaluation methods that would allow us to honour our partnership approach, as well as help us live our feminist values, which are explored further below. As part of living these values, we were challenged to strike a balance between 'upward' accountability to Oxfam and back-donors, and 'downward', or social accountability, to partners and women constituents. Where possible, it was important that we created space for co-designing monitoring and evaluations processes with partners and their constituents. At the same time, there was a need to be able to build some common understanding across the diverse stakeholders (partners, allies, Oxfam staff, and donors) about how all the pieces of this complex programme fit together, while still respecting contextual differences in the way the programme would likely unfold.

Another challenge that we faced related to the issue of reporting on predetermined results laid out in a logical framework that was part of the contractual agreement with our donor, CIDA. For both accountability and our own learning purposes, there was a need to show results at multiple levels. At the level of changes within partner organisations, we needed to demonstrate the outcomes of Oxfam Canada's capacity-building support; and at the constituent level we wanted to demonstrate changes in women's and men's lives to which partner programmes had contributed. We understood fully that in this type of capacity-building programme attempting to demonstrate cause and effect relationships of our impact would be next to impossible. That said, Oxfam and its donor CIDA wanted to be able to uncover the contributions of programme interventions to changes at different levels. Importantly, there was also onus on Oxfam Canada to provide evidence of the ways in which changes at the level of partner organisations had contributed to stronger partner programmes and programme outcomes on gender equality and women's rights – what has been referred to as the 'missing-middle' (Watkins 2004, 22) in relation to linking investments in gender mainstreaming to impacts on gender equality. While Oxfam Canada supports the view that building strong, effective, gender-just organisations is a development outcome in its own right, both Oxfam and our partners were nonetheless concerned to learn about the contribution of our capacity-building activities in supporting partners to foster changes with their constituents.

Finally, the main evaluation challenge we faced was that the EC programme sought to support 'transformative' changes; that is, structural and institutional changes in gender power relations that were built on a feminist analysis of the factors that contribute to gender inequality and injustice. We knew that we had to bring a focus on gender inequality and power relationships to the heart of our monitoring and evaluation work. In this regard, we grappled with a number of questions. How would we know transformative change if we saw it? How could we capture the complex and non-linear nature of change in gender power relations (and other power relations) both at the level of organisational change, and in women's lives? How could we ensure that the knowledge and data generated reflected the context-specificity of gender power relations? How could we develop hypotheses about how change happens that were defined enough to guide us in programme implementation and learning but not so rigid as to confine the potential of our programme? We knew that gender-sensitive approaches to evaluation could offer a lot in terms of ensuring that women were made visible in evaluation practices. However, the tools available did not seem so relevant for a 'stand-alone' gender-equality and women's rights programme,[2] which by definition would primarily focus on how the programme was being experienced by women and their families. Fortunately, as part of broader organisational efforts to 'live the values' of gender justice, Oxfam Canada was receptive to experimenting with using feminist principles to guide evaluation practice.[3]

The following sections explore how we attempted to respond to the challenges identified above by applying feminist evaluation principles in monitoring, evaluating, and learning about the EC programme. The first section describes our understanding of feminist evaluation. Then we describe briefly the EC 'feminist learning system', followed by three concrete examples of our efforts to infuse feminist principles into our evaluation practice. The final section offers some reflections on lessons learned that may be of relevance to others facing similar evaluation challenges.

Feminist evaluation

The term 'feminist evaluation' emerged about ten years ago in the evaluation community (Seigart and Brisolara 2002), and has only recently received attention in the international development context (e.g. Batliwala and Pittman 2010; Hay 2012; Podems 2010).[4] There is no one agreed upon definition of feminist evaluation; however, the Encyclopedia of Evaluation (Seigart 2005, 154–5) puts forward six tenets of feminist evaluation:

- A central concern is that *gender inequalities lead to social injustice.*
- Discrimination or inequality based on gender is *structural and systematic.*
- *Evaluation is political*; the contexts in which evaluation operates are politicised; and the personal experiences, attitudes, and characteristics that evaluators bring to evaluations (and with which we interact) lead to a particular political stance.
- Knowledge is a powerful resource that serves an explicit or implicit purpose. *Knowledge should be a resource* of and for the people who create, own, and share it.
- Knowledge and values are *culturally, socially, and temporally contingent.* Knowledge is also filtered through the knower.
- There are *many ways of knowing*; some ways are privileged over others.

As we grappled with how to bring these principles to our evaluation practice, we discovered that there appeared to be no specific feminist evaluation 'methods' distinct from other evaluation approaches. Instead, it is useful to see feminist evaluation as an overall approach or 'lens', that builds on developments within feminist research and theory of the past two decades. Like feminist research, understanding and analysing women's lived experiences from their own perspectives is the starting point for feminist evaluation, and what lends it rigour and validity. Voice and representation of women (and different groups of women) are central in this approach to evaluation, as are a firm understanding of context, and context-specific perceptions of reality. This type of evaluation includes an awareness that measures of programme 'success' may be context-specific. Not surprisingly, a common theme in literature on feminist evaluation is the importance of using participatory processes. In feminist evaluation, participation is not just about voices being represented, but rather creating space for consciousness-raising, reflexivity, and capacity building. Evaluation processes are as important as evaluation findings in feminist evaluation.

In feminist evaluation, the role of the evaluator shifts from primarily providing technical expertise to facilitating collaborative processes that are empowering and contribute to a sense of ownership for stakeholders. Knowledge and understanding become resources to be created and owned by participants in evaluation processes. How the evaluation is conducted, the way evaluators, programme staff and programme participants relate to each other, how decisions are made, are all important in a feminist evaluation (Beardsley and Miller 2002). More recent understanding of feminist evaluation pays attention to capturing incremental changes, holding the line, or even reversals in women's status as part of the complexity of challenging and changing gender power relations. Srilatha Batliwala and Alexandra Pittman's (2010) work on feminist assessment points to the need for approaches that take into account that change that is multi-dimensional involves multiple actors, and happens over a longer time-frame than many other types of international development programme interventions.

It could be said that much of what is called 'gender-sensitive' evaluation follows the same principles of feminist evaluation, given that a focus on 'gender' emerges from feminist research and theory. We would argue that this depends on two factors: first, the extent to which gender-sensitive evaluation pays attention to changes in gender power relations; and, second, how far it promotes the use of evaluation processes that are themselves empowering for stakeholders. In international development evaluation, gender-sensitive evaluation often involves integrating gender analysis into the programme design, and then collecting sex-disaggregated data as part of the monitoring process, exploring gender-differentiated programme outcomes for women and men in evaluation (see examples shared in Batliwala and Pitman 2010; United Nations Evaluation Group 2011). While this is important, gender-sensitive evaluation can be descriptive of gender-differentiated roles and relations without necessarily placing a direct emphasis on challenging and changing gender power relations (Podems 2010). Likewise, gender-sensitive evaluation does not necessarily focus on creating spaces for stakeholders to engage directly and take some ownership over the evaluation process. Of course, much depends on the evaluator or the evaluation team and there are many evaluators who bring a feminist lens and gender analysis to their evaluative work, even if they do not use the term 'feminist' evaluation (Bheda 2011).

A feminist learning system

We refer to the approach that evolved in monitoring and evaluating the EC programme, a 'feminist learning system'.[5] This term reflects the nature of this learning system, which we suggest is a methodological merging of some feminist evaluation principles with a few key elements of 'developmental evaluation'. Developmental evaluation is an approach that focuses on developing ongoing feedback loops to capture feedback from programme stakeholders and support the continuous integration of this feedback into the programme during programme implementation, as a way of placing learning at the centre of evaluative processes (Patton 2011).

The feminist learning system aspired to be an interconnected, non-linear system that responded to the need for programmatic monitoring and evaluation that was simple and flexible, reflecting our partners' realities, and centred on learning whilst maintaining the ability to meet back-donor accountability requirements. The system consisted of five key components. These were: a theory of change; a primarily quantitative performance measurement framework; evaluative moments that included a mid-term learning review, case studies, and a final evaluation; reflective spaces and sense-making exercises; and social accountability surveys.

In each of these components, we attempted to infuse the principles of feminist evaluation. Taken together, the components of the system worked as a mixed-methods approach that involved the aggregation of quantitative data, mainly through surveys, complemented with a number of qualitative methods to deepen understanding of how the programme was being experienced by stakeholders. Data from the different sources were triangulated to build a narrative of the programme's performance story.

Below, we explore in more detail three components: the theory of change; a reflective space created through a capacity assessment exercise; and a formal evaluation moment, the case studies.

Using a theory of change

From the outset, the EC programme was framed using a logical model and performance measurement framework, developed as part of the agreement with our donor, CIDA.[6] The logical model described a set of activities, outputs, and immediate and intermediate outcomes that we hoped would be achieved in the programme. However, we felt there was a need to create a more dynamic and iterative theory of change to articulate how change happens in relation to building stronger, gender-just organisations, and how changes at the organisational level contribute to gender-just changes at the societal level. It was important, we believed, to have an overarching theory of change to guide this complex programme, but we knew from the experience of past programmes that changing gender power relationships is a complex undertaking that does not follow a linear path. Therefore, the theory of change would have to be one which emphasised this view, and our methods would have to be flexible, and so able to capture the ways in which the programme unfolded in a more iterative way than was possible with the logical model. Our aim was to articulate an understanding of how change happens, and an approach to charting change, which were flexible enough to make sense to our diverse partners, their different capacities and contexts with regard to gender equality and women's rights, and their distinct stages of organisational development.

After a series of participatory exercises held across the organisation and with some partner organisations, we emerged with two theories of change. The first focused on the role of civil society organisations in supporting gender-just social change and, related to that, the importance of strong, Southern-based NGOs and networks in pushing for changes to policy and practice in their own regional and country contexts. The second theory of change, focusing on organisational change, posited that organisations become more effective change agents related to gender equality and women's rights when their own structures, policies, procedures, and programming are also democratic and gender-just. The first theory of change justified our programmatic focus on organisational capacity building, while the second provided an overarching framework for the range of tailored organisational capacity-building initiatives supported through the programme with each partner organisation. The latter described a set of capacity domains, that is, individual and organisation skills, behaviours, and resources, that we believed contributed to building stronger, gender-just organisations (Oxfam Canada 2012a, 2012b).

While there was some, quite understandable, concern among some Oxfam staff about the attempts to simplify the complexity of our programming in the form of a theory of change, there was also a real need to ensure that staff and partners across the programme were able to have some common language with which to speak about the EC programme and how we expected it would contribute to positive change in gender relations and support women's empowerment. This was to become of particular relevance when it came to telling the story of how the programme was working across the full breadth of the programme. In fact, we mapped the dimensions of our organisational theory of change on to the logical framework for the programme that had been developed as part of our contract with CIDA, in order to create a better synergy between our more dynamic vision of the programme and the outputs and outcomes laid out in the logical framework.[7] In this way, the theory of change provided a reference point for the formulation of a learning strategy, and the development of key evaluation questions to guide learning throughout programme implementation. It provided programme staff and partners with a starting point for discussions about how the programme was being experienced, and the contributions it was making in a variety of areas.

About mid-way through the programme, Oxfam undertook a 'sense-making review' of the organisational theory of change involving a process to create shared understanding from different perspectives, building on a huge amount of programme information, to make sense of how the programme was unfolding in different contexts. The exercise explored the extent to which the theory of change developed at the beginning of the programme was supported by evidence emerging from programme implementation.

Two key outcomes resulted from the sense-making exercise. First, the organisational theory of change was validated in that evidence was available to support the hypothesised relationship between internal organisational transformation and gender-just programmatic outcomes. However, the exercise also demonstrated a need to refine the original articulation of the theory of change to bring into greater focus some missing ingredients that were perceived to contribute to supporting gender-just organisational change, including, for example, women's transformative leadership. Importantly, the re-articulation of the theory of change was refined on the basis of perspectives that emerged on how gender-just organisational change happens that were the outcome of participatory processes that supported partners to reflect on their experiences of building gender-just organisations. However, reconstructing the theory of change to incorporate this learning also presented challenges for programme monitoring. Back-donor reporting remained tied to the original logical framework, and data collected in relation to the re-framed theory of change needed to be carefully transposed to that framework, which was time-consuming for staff. In summary, we found that using a theory of change helped us to be clearer on our assumptions about the relationship between our capacity-building programming strategies and their intended outcomes. It was also the basis for engaging programme stakeholders in learning processes throughout the programme, and engaging them to shift programming strategies and re-articulate programme outcomes in ways that were more meaningful to them.

Capacity assessment and benchmarking tool

The Capacity Assessment and Benchmarking Tool – known as the CAT by Oxfam Canada staff and partners – was designed as a participatory self-assessment exercise around which EC partners could identify needs and design a context-specific capacity-building strategy to support them in becoming stronger, gender-just organisations. Some components of the strategy were then funded by the EC programme, but the strategy itself was owned by partners and used by some of them to create inputs into their organisational development plans (see Oxfam Canada 2012b). In keeping with Oxfam Canada's

partnership principles as well as feminist evaluation principles, it was important that the CAT process engaged partners in self-reflection and assessment,
rather than being conducted as a third-party needs assessment exercise. The
CAT approach honoured the experience and perspectives that participants
brought to the exercise, and engaged them in a conversation about current
organisational capacities versus desired capacities needed to undertake effective gender-just work.

While the CAT self-assessment method enables multiple perspectives to surface, its effective use requires skilled facilitation, with some foreknowledge of
existing power relations within an organisation, and strategies for how these
can be managed to create space for different voices to be heard. The CAT has
enabled a wide array of deeply sensitive issues to surface about gender power
relations that may inhibit partners' paths to becoming gender-just organisations. For example, for some partners the CAT exercise led them to reflect on
the numbers of women in senior management positions, or to question the
disconnect between gender policy commitments and organisational practices,
particularly with regard to work–life balance. For others, the CAT enabled
them to delve deeper into how far they believed they were 'living the values'
of gender justice, in relation to ways of working and relating within their
organisation. Organisations also reflected on what transformative women's
leadership meant and felt like, and how far the programmes they designed
and implemented were focused on transformative changes in gender power
relations.

The CAT generates both quantitative and qualitative data about current
capacity areas and desired areas for improvement. From these, we can create
a picture of these issues at the 'baseline', which enables partners to carry out
self-monitoring over time. During the EC programme, these self-assessment
scores were re-visited and reflected upon each year. Partners' experience with
the CAT has been mainly positive. As noted by one participant:

> The capacity building exercise is extremely useful … it helps us to track prog-
> ress and identify capacity gaps on our own. (Anonymous questionnaire,
> Keystone Accountability, August 2011, 19)

Feedback from partners suggests that intentionally revisiting and reassessing
capacity to work on particular issues, and linking this to an analysis of gender
power relations in our own organisations, allows each partner the opportunity
to own the self-assessment process, and have an honest conversation about
areas of progress as well as set-backs and reversals.

The CAT is an example of designing evaluative processes that meet the
learning and accountability needs of multiple stakeholders. In addition to providing baseline information for individual partners' self-monitoring, the CAT
enabled Oxfam Canada to aggregate quantitative data and track trends across
the entire set of EC programme partners throughout the five-year programme.
The data provided the basis for comparative analysis across different types of

programme partners and across regions. For example, we noticed at the beginning of the programme that women's and feminist organisations seemed to have a more inherently self-critical bias and tended to rate themselves lower in their self-assessments of internal capacities, compared to other types of NGOs, even in relation to living the values of gender justice. This finding was particularly intriguing because staff observations were that feminist organisations tended to have a more firmly rooted transformative perspective to gender power relations already present within their organisations. We saw this trend reverse about mid-way through the programme, when many NGOs engaged in Gender Action Learning (GAL).[8] The GAL process helped partners engage in a more profound analysis of what it meant to be an organisation that lived the values of gender justice, ultimately leading to a lower self-assessment score in the CAT exercise than they had previously rated themselves. Related to this, the CAT provided a basis for partners to reflect on blockages or reversals in their organisational capacities, for example, the impact of turnover of staff with gender expertise, or changes in leadership.

Engendering change case studies

Throughout the EC programme, Oxfam Canada engaged in formal evaluation exercises, including formative and summative evaluations as well as a series of case studies. These processes have helped us to further explore our theory of change and synthesise and deepen learning around key outcomes of the programme. The case studies were conducted in response to the need to explore and understand the 'missing middle', of how changes at the organisational level were creating impacts at the beneficiary level, especially in the lives of girls and women.

While the EC programme was working in partnership with 44 different organisations, we decided to do a purposeful sampling of three partners to create 'information- rich' case studies that we thought would help yield greater nuance and depth about changing gender power relationships both at the organisational and beneficiary levels (Patton 2002, 181). Although Oxfam Canada put forward a set of four guiding questions that united the case studies, each took shape in different ways in large part because the processes were co-designed by the participating partners, reflecting their own contexts, geographic focus, and programmatic issues. Each partner also included their own learning question to guide the case study and was able to co-design a written or video output for each of the cases.

Importantly, it was agreed with partners that the approach to the case studies would explicitly incorporate some guiding principles of feminist evaluation. In particular, this meant that we would focus on learning to enhance our collective understanding of the power relationships that had been challenged and changed within the EC programme. This also required the process of the case studies to shift the traditional power structure of the monitoring and evaluation by allowing our partners and some of their beneficiaries to be in the driver's seat in terms of the design of the process, the data collection, analysis, and validation of the data collected. The key role of the consultants and Oxfam staff was to support and facilitate the process, convening training workshops, synthesising the information, and presenting it to stakeholders in the form of videos – which is discussed further below.

In all three case studies, we collectively decided to use adaptations of the most-significant change (MSC) technique. We decided to do this because it was participatory, and partners all agreed it was easier for beneficiaries to tell stories of change than to talk about 'indicators' linked to specific outcomes. All case studies started with building the capacity of partner staff, as well as some beneficiaries from their programmes, so that they could use MSC. In one case, this took the shape of partner staff and their beneficiaries learning how to interview each other first and then conducting similar interviews with a variety of other beneficiaries in their programmes. Instead of documenting with written notes, we used video to capture the interviews. Partner staff and volunteers conducting the interviews themselves not only built their evaluation capacity, it also helped ensure that the interviews were more culturally appropriate and accommodated language differences (Peer Associates 2013). In another case study, staff and beneficiaries were introduced to the methodology 'Photo Voice'. Using this technique meant that significant change stories were first designed on story boards, and then staff and beneficiaries were asked to go back into their communities, use digital cameras, and create photo essays of the top four change stories they had identified in their communities (see Evallab 2013).

In all cases, a participatory workshop was held approximately one month after the stories were gathered, where partners and beneficiaries were able to reflect together on information collected, discuss key themes, and make sense of the information. This workshop also provided the opportunity for participants to ensure that the story in the case study accurately reflected their organisations' experience in the EC programme. Feedback from partners about the case study process has been mainly positive; in fact we have heard from partners that they did not know monitoring, evaluation, and learning could be so 'fun'. Because partners and beneficiaries were involved right from the beginning of the process, they have found the information collected was particularly useful and are excited about the videos that were generated from the process.

The learning generated from the case studies also helped Oxfam and partners deepen our understanding of some of the significant outcomes of our work in terms of changes at community, household, and individual beneficiary level, outcomes to which the EC programme contributed. The case studies demonstrated the key role that women's and girls' empowerment and leadership play in challenging and changing gender power relationships, but generated surprising empowerment outcome measurements not intended by our EC partner or Oxfam. For example, at the community level, women beneficiaries In the Matabeleland Region of Zimbabwe focused on the acquisition of new assets such as a teapot, cups, and livestock as a significant sign of independence and empowerment. Both men and women beneficiaries spoke of enhanced interpersonal relationships, but suggested weight gain, enjoyment of sexual relations, and increased fidelity in marriages as key indicators of improvements in gender relations. As noted by a partner staff member,

> the main differences [in how empowerment is measured] are that the staff have a more holistic and broader picture of what empowerment looks like ... constituents spoke to individual issues of economic empowerment and acquiring assets, but also the angle of interpersonal relationships and improvement in the household. (Interview in Peer Associates 2013, 18)

The different ways in which programme outcomes were described by constituents underscores the strength and relevance of the MSC methodology, as discussing changes by way of storytelling allowed relevant and culturally appropriate indicators of success to emerge.

For many women interviewed in the case studies, the development of their leadership at a professional level has also created a sense of empowerment in their personal life. This was as true for staff members in our partner organisations, as for programme beneficiaries. Many women remarked that assuming a leadership role outside of the home has brought greater respect for them within their communities and even within their homes. For example, staff from our EC partner in Zimbabwe reported improved marriages and better communications with their husbands, as well as being able to broach topics like HIV/AIDS with their children (Peer Associates 2013). Staff interviewed emphasised a sense of consistency and authenticity across different aspects of their lives: the shift in gender imbalances at the organisational level, the work in which they engage to challenge gender inequality at the community level; and shifts in power relationships at the personal level. As one partner staff member remarked:

> I personally believe I am the change I want to see in the world and if I want to see engendering change, the change has to start with me. Every moment is a time for me to learn. (Interview in Peer Associates 2013, 12)

The case studies also demonstrated that often the programme entry point is focused on women community members, for example in income-generating groups that integrate awareness raising on women's rights, but in order to challenge and change gender power relationships successfully, a whole community approach is required. For example, in Ethiopia there is a community-oriented gender-based violence monitoring group that consists of women representatives from self-help groups, local governmental officials, police, and traditional leaders. This monitoring group has meant that women have a safe space to go when violence occurs and are able to receive guidance and support. The gender-based violence monitoring group has also helped reduce the harmful traditional practice of 'early marriage' in the community. According to beneficiaries interviewed, the reduction of child marriages has also meant that young girls are staying in school longer. Locally grounded notions of changing gender power relations also emerged from the case studies. For example, some partners described gender equality as creating more balance of power and space for women rather than inversing power dynamics. Moreover, the inclusion of men in programming has been important in shifting power imbalances and space for women. As stated by one partner staff member

> *the inclusion of men is critical to any women's rights programme because gender equality questions dynamics that exist. We live in a patriarchal society so men hold the power. So when we include them, it is about creating space, asking men to sift off some power...* (Interview in Peer Associates 2013, 8)

Feminist evaluation principles reminded us that we had to be more explicit about documenting evidence of unanticipated outcomes, specifically evidence of resistance, backlash, and seemingly negative changes as indicators of 'successfully' challenging gender power relationships. An example of resistance that was unearthed during the Zimbabwean case study was that while men were sometimes open to assuming certain tasks stereotypically assumed by women, these roles were not always accepted by others in the community. For example, men reported taking sick children to health centres, but discovered that health-care professionals would not accept a child without her or his mother. This example suggests that acceptance from formal institutions, laws, and practices is often important for individual behaviours, norms, and practices to be accepted and changed in ways that are sustainable. While many interviewees relayed stories of success related to women's leadership, there were also some examples of resistance. In both Ethiopia and Zimbabwe, women community members noted that they are still not taken seriously with police and at local courts when attempting to seek justice after experiencing gender-based violence. At both the beneficiary and organisational levels, women noted not being given credit for hard work or, having to work harder than men to prove their leadership skills. Similarly, women at the organisational and community levels felt that the women who successfully assumed leadership roles are required to take on 'male' characteristics like being aggressive, firm, decisive, which they felt reinforced gender stereotypes rather than creating a different type of leadership.

Reflections and lessons learned

Our efforts to support staff and partners to tell the performance story of the EC programme required a constant revisiting of the theory of change we are using, as well as experimenting with innovative approaches and methods that would capture both transformative changes within partner organisations as well as in the lives of women that partner programming reached. The approaches we took were shaped both by the external aid environment with its results orientation as well as by our aspirations to bring feminist principles to our monitoring and evaluation practice. Below, we share some of the key lessons learned.

Getting the process right

A central feature in allowing principles of feminist evaluation to shape our monitoring and evaluation was a strong emphasis on getting the process right. This approach required us to honour the knowledge, context, and experience of our partners, which logically led to the use of participatory tools and methods. The use of participatory processes and co-design elements led to stronger local ownership amongst stakeholders over the evaluative process itself. Related to this was the need to invest in capacity building with partners and constituents to strengthen their skills in using evaluative methods. For example, in the case studies, the co-design of the evaluation included capacity building with local stakeholders on conducting MSC interviews and analysing the data they collected. Within the CAT process, partners were supported to use a self-assessment technique to track their own progress and explore challenges they faced in becoming stronger, gender-just organisations. These processes reflect a shift in power relationships from partners having monitoring and evaluation conducted 'on' them to evaluations being 'with and for' partners. Implicit within this shift is allowing partners to guide the process and for Oxfam to be open to having the process unfold differently than anticipated. Getting the process right also created different criteria for what counts as evidence, in that it places a high value in reflecting stakeholders' lived experience of the programme. The examples shared here are also illustrative of a shift in the role and skills of the evaluator, with more emphasis on playing the role of a critical friend than on the notion of an objective, technical expert. Oxfam's role as critical friend required us to facilitate, listen, and be attentive to unanticipated results which require space for open conversation and wider exploration. One of the key lessons from engaging in these types of processes is that they require considerable time investment both for Oxfam and our partners. They worked best with partners who were also committed to putting the guiding principles to feminist evaluation into practice, strengthening their internal monitoring and evaluation capacity, and experimenting with and engaging in participatory processes to collect and analyse programme information.

Respecting diversity and context

Many development interventions now take a programmatic approach which contributes to shifting power into the hands of external planners, strategists, and evaluators (Wallace *et al.* 2013). Oxfam's commitment to working in partnership to support a diverse group of Southern organisations to design and deliver locally relevant programmes contributed to the strength of the EC programme; however, as we have described above, this created the challenging need to aggregate data that was context- and partner-specific. We tried to respond to this challenge by using a variety of participatory evaluation methods throughout the programme that enabled context- and partner-specific experiences of the programme to emerge. The CAT, for example, created space for very diverse partners to identify where they were on their pathways to becoming gender-just organisations and to tailor capacity-building strategies that responded to their specific needs. The annual self-assessment processes tracked changes over time relative to a partner's unique starting point. Wherever possible, we aggregated information emerging from participatory assessment processes to tell the whole programme performance story. We also used this feedback to revise our theory of change to bring it closer to how changes were being experienced in the programme.

Another key lesson was the value of using case studies to explore the complexity of how social change happens. Given time and resource constraints, we could not have done this type of extensive exercise with more than three partners, and the effort to select which partners to involve was a prolonged and at times difficult process. In a programme of 44 partners, it is fair to say that three case studies are not representative of the entire programme. This underscores the importance of having multiple sources of information to triangulate (that is, cross-check) data, a fact we have recognised and integrated into our feminist learning system. Nonetheless it is important to emphasise that using case studies enabled a much deeper, nuanced analysis that otherwise would have been impossible. It allowed us to explore in a context- and partner-specific manner the complex ways in which capacity-building support at the partner organisational level influenced changes in how partners did programming on gender equality and women's rights and in turn how these contributed to outcomes for partner programme constituents. In particular, by using the participatory validation exercise, partners and some beneficiaries were able to discuss, reflect, and make sense of the generated data. This exercise ensured that the case studies enabled context-specific outcomes and indicators to be surfaced and prioritised. Case study data were analysed and synthesised across partner organisations to draw out general points wherever possible, while still holding on to the value of contextual understanding.

Embracing complexity

Within the context of the current aid environment there is pressure to tell a positive, simple story that demonstrates programme impact, preferably backed up by numbers. As others have pointed out, telling the story of changes in women's lives is complex and messy (Batliwala and Pittman 2010; Wallace *et al.* 2013). As we have described above, the evaluation approaches used for the EC programme sought to embrace complexity rather than generalise and simplify it. The various evaluative processes created space to capture non-linear change experienced by programme stakeholders, including backsliding on previous gains as well as encountering resistance to change. We took a dynamic approach to our theory of change which we revisited and revised as the programme unfolded. While the theory of change provided some degree of programme coherence, it did not act as a straitjacket. Given the range of partners and the diversity of those partner's own constituents, we were unable to move beyond the level of partners in trying to build some shared ownership of this complex, multi-region programme. However, we tried to honour the outcomes that partners and stakeholders identified as most important even when they did not fit neatly within our own theory of change. Of course, we still faced challenges synching our flexible theory of change with the programme's logical framework which remained more static.

Balancing learning and accountability

Like many other NGOs, at Oxfam Canada we have found it a struggle to strike a balance between learning and accountability. An important lesson for us has been to try to develop approaches that meet accountability needs of multiple stakeholders. We tried to use different approaches that helped us to meet our accountability to our back-donor CIDA but still prioritised the engagement of our partners in participatory exercises to meet their needs. We achieved this to some extent with the CAT which provided data for partners' ongoing monitoring as well as for the performance measurement framework on which we reported aggregated programme results to our back-donor. Using the theory of a change as a guide, we tried to be strategic in focusing programme learning to build our collective understanding about how gender power relationships were being challenged and changed. In particular, certain processes like the CAT and case studies helped us make sense of non-linear results like resistance and backlash that often occur when gender power relations are challenged. Of course, other learning happened in the programme on an on-going basis but having this focus helped us move out of our comfort zone of activity reporting towards being able say something with confidence about outcomes to which the programme had contributed.

In some areas, we fell short in our aspirations with regard to applying feminist evaluation principles. In spite of our efforts, there was probably still too much upward reporting by partners to meet broader accountability requirements, which speaks to the fundamental power relationships at play.[9] We did not have the resources to engage with all partners in certain exercises, particularly in the case studies, which in our view were the most successful experiment in bringing feminist evaluation principles into practice. However, our efforts to embrace feminist evaluation principles encouraged us to think differently about how we engage ourselves and our partners in evaluation. It supported us to dig a bit more deeply at understanding how gender power relations change and to understand what those changes looked like from the perspective of stakeholders. Most importantly, however, feminist evaluation principles reminded us of whose voices matter most in evaluation and whose stories should count as credible evidence of results.

Notes

1. This chapter is written from the perspectives of two MEAL staff members who self-identify as feminists. Their efforts to bring feminist values and principles to evaluative processes was strongly supported by many colleagues, including the Director of the Centre for Gender Justice, Caroline Marrs, and the Executive Director of Oxfam Canada, Robert Fox. Overall, Oxfam Canada was receptive to experimenting with feminist principles in its efforts to 'live the values' of gender justice in its organisational culture and ways of working.

2. We use the term 'stand-alone' gender equality and women's rights programmes to differentiate them from programmes in which gender is 'mainstreamed'. For the first, the programme focus is already on gender equality and women's rights though the extent to which power relations are addressed depends on the specific programme. For the second, the programme may not overtly address gender equality and women's rights concerns and as a result attention to gender-related issues and outcomes need to be mainstreamed into the programme – hence the term 'gender mainstreaming'.

3. In 2006, Oxfam Canada took the decision to focus its organisational mandate on gender equality and women's rights. As part of that process it undertook a gender audit, the findings of which included some recommendations to enable the organisation to 'walk the talk' on gender justice, including its monitoring and evaluation work. Recently, Oxfam Canada used the Capacity Assessment and Benchmarking Tool (CAT) exercise internally (see Oxfam Canada 2009).

4. A report by Batliwala and Pittman (2010) for the Association for Women's Rights in Development provides a good overview of the challenges faced by evaluators in attempting to 'capture change in women's realities', including the non-linear nature of change. The authors present some principles for feminist assessment as a basis for feminist evaluation. The chapter by Podems (2010) provides a description of both feminist evaluation and of a gender approach to evaluation and explores them in the historical context of the development of gender analysis in international development and human rights work. Hay's (2012) article examines how feminist theory and practice is influencing the framing, methods, and conduct of evaluation in India and argues that, in the face of a narrowing of what is considered 'robust' development evaluation, feminist evaluation must demonstrate its rigour and play a stronger role in supporting us to understand how societies change. Here it is worth noting that Oxfam International hosted a learning event in June 2013 where 35 gender justice practitioners from across the confederation reflected on their experiences and agreed the value of feminist evaluation principles to guide their evaluation practice.

5. It was only towards the end of the programme that the term 'feminist learning system' was used by Oxfam staff to describe the learning approach that had evolved during the course of the programme implementation, though Oxfam Canada consciously promoted 'feminist evaluation principles' with many partners and stakeholders throughout the programme.

6. Accompanying all CIDA-funded programmes is a results-based management logical framework, noted above, as well as a performance measurement framework which assigns indicators, baseline data, targets, data sources, data collection methods, frequency, and responsibility for the pre-determined outputs and outcomes. When we refer to a logical model we mean both of these performance measurement techniques.
7. For example, we used changes in the capacity domains from our theory of change as indicators for the immediate outcomes in the logical framework.
8. Gender Action Learning is a methodology developed by Gender at Work to address the gap between gender equality policies and deeply held cultural norms that are manifest in everyday unequal power relations within organisations. The approach allows participating organisations to question their assumptions about gender and other internalised norms that negatively affect their ability to live the values of gender and diversity. See http://www.genderatwork.org/OurWork/OurPrograms/GenderAction-LearningGAL.aspx (last checked by the authors May 2014).
9. While we perhaps placed too much emphasis on upward accountability, we did attempt to integrate mechanisms of 'downward' or social accountability into the programme. To review the anonymous feedback Oxfam Canada received from partners on its performance in the areas of financial and programme support, administration, communications, monitoring, reporting, and learning, see Keystone Accountability (2011).

References

Batliwala, Srilatha and Alexandra Pittman (2010) *Capturing Change in Women's Realities: A Critical Overview of Current Monitoring & Evaluation Frameworks and Approaches*, Toronto: Association for Women's Rights in Development, http://www.awid.org/About-AWID/AWID-News/Capturing-Change-in-Women-s-Realities (last checked by the authors May 2014).

Beardsley, Rebecca M. and MichelleHuges Miller (2002) 'Revisioning the process: a case study in feminist programme evaluation', *New Directions in Evaluation* 96: 57–70.

Bheda, Divya (2011) 'En "gendering" evaluation: feminist evaluation but "I am NOT a feminist!"', *New Directions for Evaluation* 131: 53–58.

Evallab (2013) *Engendering Change Case Studies*: Ethiopia, http://go.oxfam.ca/docs/ec-case-studies/ethiopia/ec-case-study-final-report-2013-08.pdf (last checked by the authors May 2014).

Gonzalez Manchón, Beatriz and Morna Macleod (2010) 'Challenging gender inequality in famers' organisations in Nicaragua', *Gender and Development* 18(3): 373–86.

Hay, Katherine (2012) 'Engendering policies and programmes through feminist evaluation: opportunities and insights', *Indian Journal of Gender Studies* 19(2): 321–40.

Keystone Accountability (2011) Partner Feedback Report: Oxfam Canada. *Keystone Performance Surveys*: INGO Partner Survey, London: Keystone Accountability, http://oxfam.ca/sites/default/files/imce/partner_survey_oxfam_english_2011.pdf (last checked by the authors May 2014).

Oxfam Canada (2009) *Summary Report of the Oxfam Canada Gender Audit*, Ottawa: Oxfam Canada, http://oxfam.ca/our-work/publications/publications-and-reports/walking-the-talk (last checked by the authors May 2014).

Oxfam Canada (2012a) *The Power of Gender-Just organisations: Framework for Transformative Organisational Capacity Building for Gender Justice*, Ottawa: Oxfam Canada, http://www.oxfam.ca/sites/default/files/Ox-Gender-Framework_final-web.pdf (last checked by the authors May 2014).

Oxfam Canada (2012b) *The Power of Gender-Just organisations: Toolkit for Transformative Organisational Capacity Building*, Ottawa: Oxfam Canada, http://www.oxfam.ca/sites/default/files/Ox-Gender-Toolkit_web-final_0.pdf (last checked by the authors May 2014).

Patton, Michael Quinn (2002) *Qualitative Research and Evaluation Methods*, third edition, London: Sage Publications.

Patton, Michael Quinn (2011) *Developmental Evaluation: Applying Complexity Concepts to Enhance Innovation and Use*, New York: The Guildford Press.

Peer Associates (2013) *Engendering Change: Zimbabwe Case Study*, http://go.oxfam.ca/docs/ec-case-studies/ec-case-study-zimbabwe.pdf (last checked by the authors May 2014).

Podems, Donna R. (2010) 'Feminist evaluation and gender approaches: there's a difference?', *Journal of Multidisciplinary Evaluation* 6(14): 1–17, http://www.jmde.com/ (last checked by the authors May 2014).

Seigart, Denise (2005) 'Feminist evaluation', in Sandra Mathison (ed.) Encylopedia of Evaluation, Thousand Oaks, CA: Sage, pp. 154–157.

Seigart, Denise and Sharon Brisolara (2002) 'Special Issue: Feminist evaluation: explorations and experiences', *New Directions in Evaluation* 96: 1–114.

United Nations Evaluation Group (2011) *Integrating Human Rights and Gender Equality in Evaluation: Towards UNEG Guidance* http://www.unesco.org/new/fileadmin/MULTIME-DIA/HQ/IOS/temp/HRGE%20Handbook.pdf (last checked by the authors May 2014).

Wallace, Tina, Fenella Porter, and Mark Ralph-Bowman (2013) *Aid, NGOs and the realities of Women's Lives: A Perfect Storm*, Bourton on Dunsmore, Rugby: Practical Action Publishing.

Watkins, Francis (2004) *'Evaluation of DFID Development Assistance: Gender Equality and Women's Empowerment. DFID's Experience of Gender Mainstreaming 1995–2004'*, Glasgow: DFID.

About the authors

Carol Miller is an evaluation specialist for the Oxfam Knowledge Hub on Gender-Based Violence, Centre for Gender Justice, Oxfam Canada. Postal address: 39 McArthur Avenue, Ottawa, Ontario, K1L 8L7, Canada. Email: cgj@oxfam.ca.

Laura Haylock currently works as Women's Rights Officer, Gender MEL, Centre for Gender Justice, Oxfam Canada. Postal address: 39 McArthur Avenue, Ottawa, Ontario, K1L 8L7, Canada. Email: cgj@ oxfam.ca.

CHAPTER 7

A survivor behind every number: using programme data on violence against women and girls in the Democratic Republic of Congo to influence policy and practice

Marie-France Guimond and Katie Robinette

Abstract

Designing and implementing programmes that seek to respond to, and prevent, violence against women and girls (VAWG) saves lives and mitigates the consequences of such violence for survivors. With the right evidence about the scale and nature of VAWG, practitioners, donors, and policymakers can improve programming, support VAWG services where they are needed, and develop policies to address VAWG. The International Rescue Committee (IRC) is a leading international non-government organisation (NGO) with VAWG programmes in over 18 countries worldwide, and it is one of the only NGOs with a dedicated technical unit on women's protection and empowerment. It has over ten years of experience in the Democratic Republic of the Congo (DRC), a country where reports of pervasive acts of violence against women and girls have attracted significant international attention. With a strong emphasis on evidence-based and evidence-generating programming, the IRC carefully collects VAWG data as part of the services provided to up to 3,000 VAWG survivors per year in the DRC. In this paper, the IRC shares its experience on VAWG data, and how this information can be interpreted as well as how it is often misinterpreted.

Keywords: violence against women and girls, Democratic Republic of the Congo, monitoring and evaluation, policy, conflict, reporting

Introduction

Violence against women and girls (VAWG)[1] programming is life-saving, and crucial in mitigating the harmful consequences of such violence on survivors. Yet VAWG can be particularly difficult to quantify and understand: it is a largely invisible problem, with many cases never reported; its scope is difficult to estimate, even where prevalence estimates exist; and it is a sensitive issue

http://dx.doi.org/10.3362/9781780447049.007

that requires a nuanced and contextual understanding, strict guidelines on confidentiality, and adherence to ethical principles. At the same time, with the right evidence, practitioners, donors, and policymakers can improve programming, support VAWG services where they are needed, and develop policies to address VAWG effectively.

The International Rescue Committee (IRC) is a leading international non-government organisation (NGO) with VAWG programmes in over 18 countries worldwide. It is one of only a few NGOs with a dedicated technical unit on women's protection and empowerment, whose programmes facilitate the healing, dignity, and self-determination of women and girls who have experienced violence, creating opportunities for them to transform their lives and to make their voices heard in pursuit of a safer, more equitable world. The IRC has over ten years of experience in the Democratic Republic of the Congo (DRC), a country that has experienced almost two decades of conflict and where reports of pervasive acts of VAWG have attracted significant international attention. With a strong emphasis on evidence-based and evidence-generating programming, the IRC carefully collected data as part of the services provided to over 12,000 VAWG survivors in the DRC since 2009. Of these survivors of violence that have received services through the IRC, more than 99 per cent are women and girls. In this chapter, the IRC shares its experience on these data, and offers insights into how such information can be interpreted. It also highlights how data can often be misinterpreted. Its goal is to show how monitoring, evaluation, and learning on VAWG can ensure high-quality programming that responds fully to the interests and needs of women and girls in the DRC.

Understanding VAWG data: VAWG data are the visible portion of a largely invisible problem

Collected safely and ethically, contextualised service-based data on reported VAWG cases can help practitioners, donors, and policymakers improve programming, address gaps in service provision, and develop policies to address pervasive forms of violence.

Globally, only a portion of all VAWG incidents are reported to service providers (Palermo *et al.* 2013, 1–11). Even in industrialised countries, it is estimated that less than half of rape cases are reported. When making any decisions based on VAWG data, it is important to remember that these service-based data represent only the visible portion of a largely invisible problem:

> One of the characteristics of GBV [gender-based violence], and in particular
> sexual violence, is under-reporting ... Any available data, in any setting, about
> GBV reports from police, legal, health, or other sources will represent only
> a very small proportion of the actual number of incidents of GBV. (Inter-
> Agency Standing Committee 2005, 4)

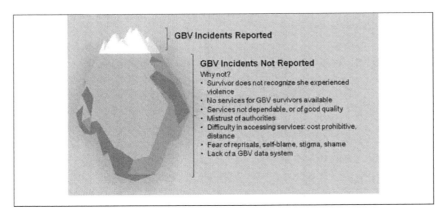

Figure 7.1 The tip of the iceberg – globally, only a portion of all cases are reported

Thankfully, good programming and good policies can be developed to address VAWG, even without exact knowledge of how many cases are occurring. Policymakers and donors can use both existing VAWG programme data, as well as lessons learned and best practices on VAWG (Figure 7.1).

Since 2011 in the DRC, the IRC has been using the Gender-Based Violence Information Management System (GBVIMS) to manage and analyse service-based data. The GBVIMS was developed by the UNFPA (United Nations Population Fund), the IRC, and the UNHCR (Office of the United Nations High Commissioner for Refugees) to harmonise VAWG data produced through service-delivery in humanitarian settings. It enables humanitarian actors responding to VAWG to safely collect, store and analyse this data, and facilitate the safe and ethical sharing of this data. The intention of the system is to assist the VAWG community to understand better the cases being reported by enabling service providers to more easily generate high-quality VAWG incident data across their programmes, properly analyse that data, and safely share it with other agencies for broader trends analysis and improved VAWG co-ordination.

While there are certainly limitations to the conclusions that can be drawn from service-based data, it is the one form of data most readily accessible in humanitarian settings over time. It can provide concrete information to inform programmes and policies, and affect the lives of survivors when reviewed regularly and understood in the context in which it was collected.

How can we ensure that VAWG incidents are reported to service providers?

First and foremost, specialised services to respond to VAWG should be available. The IRC's experience is that VAWG survivors tend to report incidents only when there are specialised services for VAWG. In the DRC during the emergency in North Kivu in late 2012, which caused widespread population displacement, many general assessments in camps said that no one reported VAWG incidents during displacement or in the camps. Yet, when VAWG listening centres staffed with specially trained community members opened in the camps, survivors began to report VAWG cases on the first day the listening centre was opened – in every camp. These incidents were simply not being reported during general assessments, probably because of the lack of services available, which means that there was no tangible reason for survivors to come forward and talk about their traumatic experience.

In a functional VAWG service system, where specialised VAWG services are available and accessible and VAWG data are collected in an ethical manner, several prerequisites must be in place for survivors to come forward and report an incident of VAWG, and for this information to be fed onwards, into the overall monitoring and evaluation system of programme data. First, the VAWG survivor, through wider community information dissemination, is informed of services and where to find them. Next, the survivor makes contact with a VAWG service provider, and reports the incident while receiving services. While reporting an incident, the survivor has to provide informed consent for her (anonymised, non-identifiable) information to be shared for improved co-ordination, advocacy, or reporting. Finally, the survivor's information is compiled with other survivors' data at the service-provider level, to produce statistical reports for trend analysis.

Once VAWG services are available, it is also important to reduce barriers to accessing these services. Not only can this provide potentially life-saving support to more VAWG survivors but it also has the positive side-effect of increasing the amount of information available on VAWG in order to improve programming and policy decisions. Barriers to accessing services can happen at different levels.

Common barriers to accessing services include:

- Information: survivors may not know that specialised VAWG services are available, and may not even recognise that the violence they are experiencing is VAWG, because it is pervasive and accepted in the community. Word of mouth also matters – the IRC's experience in the DRC is that survivors are more likely to report if they have more trust in the confidentiality and the quality of VAWG services available.
- Access: access not only refers to geographic location, but also the ability to pay for services if they are not free, and the survivors' eligibility for these services. It is also important to take into consideration that survivors may be less likely to report if the service providers are male, if the service providers do not speak the local language, or, notably in DRC, if the service providers are not community members.
- Safe, confidential, and ethical data collection: international best practices state that the safety and the security of the survivor and the service provider are paramount. Especially in contexts like the DRC, where

VAWG survivors are often stigmatised and shamed, survivors are less likely to report if they believe that their confidentiality may be jeopardised. One of the core principles for VAWG service providers is to provide services with respect, empathy, and without discrimination.

Since not all VAWG cases are reported, prevalence studies can attempt to estimate how many VAWG incidents occur

Prevalence studies estimate the total number of VAWG incidents – both reported and not reported. In the iceberg analogy, they are trying to measure the whole iceberg. Prevalence studies can be very useful to provide an overall picture of VAWG in a country or area, but it is important to keep in mind that these are estimates, and can vary quite a bit depending on methodology.

Numerous studies have tried to assess the scope of VAWG in the DRC, resulting in a wide range of estimates. In a study in North and South Kivu provinces and Ituri district, Johnson et al. found that 40 per cent of women reported ever experiencing sexual violence, while Peterman et al. found that roughly 21 and 13 per cent of women reported lifetime experience of rape in North and South Kivu, respectively, and 12 per cent nationally (Johnson et al. 2010, 557; Peterman et al. 2011, 1064). The United States Government Accountability Office estimated that 9 per cent of the total population in eastern DRC had experienced sexual violence in a one-year period from 2009 to 2010 (U.S. Government Accountability Office 2011, 10), while Peterman et al. found from 2007 data that about 7 and 4 per cent of women in North and South Kivu, respectively, reported having experienced rape in the previous 12 months, and less than 3 per cent nationally (Peterman et al. 2011, 1064). Kirsten Johnson et al. found that more than 30 per cent of women reported some form of intimate partner violence, with roughly 3 per cent of respondents reporting intimate partner sexual violence (Johnson et al. 2010, 557), while the 2007 national Demographic and Health Survey in the DRC found that 71 per cent of women reported some sort of intimate partner violence, with 35 per cent reporting intimate partner sexual violence (Ministry of Planning, Democratic Republic of Congo 2008, 306).

As with all collection and analysis of VAWG data, prevalence studies should conform to international ethical research principles. One very important standard in research ethics for VAWG data is that 'basic care and support for survivors must be available locally before commencing any activity that may involve individuals disclosing information about their experiences of sexual violence' (World Health Organization 2007, 9). However, with large-scale prevalence studies, VAWG services are not always in place to support survivors who participate. Because of this, the ethical principles of VAWG data collection must be carefully weighed before asking individuals to disclose information about their experiences of violence.

Especially when combined with a larger health and demographic survey, VAWG prevalence studies may be limited in the level of detail that they are able to collect on incidents of violence. While prevalence studies can be important for giving a general estimate of the scope of violence, they usually provide little information on more subtle or short-term changes in VAWG trends, the specific needs of specific groups of survivors, or the quality of services available, which requires a nuanced understanding of the context and more detailed information on reported cases. This is where programme data and lessons learned can go a long way in completing and understanding the information collected during prevalence studies.

Using VAWG data: existing VAWG information can be very useful when analysed contextually

Understanding and using VAWG data means accepting that exact numbers on the extent of VAWG may never be available. However, this does not signify that practitioners, donors, and policymakers cannot make informed decisions. Existing VAWG information can be very useful, provided that it is analysed contextually.

When looking at reported VAWG incidents over time, it is possible to learn very valuable information about:

- The profile of VAWG survivors (demographics).
- What type of VAWG they are reporting.
- When and where the alleged incident occurred.
- The profile of the alleged perpetrator (demographics, relationship to survivor).
- Which services are available in which sites.
- Which services are most often utilised by VAWG survivors.

The next step to analysing compiled reported VAWG data is to look at it contextually. It is crucial to remember that these numbers come from a particular setting – service providers in a particular geographic area; and that behind every number is a survivor with a specific story. Any analysis of VAWG data should be coupled with the expertise of service providers on the setting where services are provided. The data could also be complemented by other sources of VAWG data, such as programme data from other service providers, prevalence studies, or qualitative studies.

Throughout the IRC's ten years of work on VAWG services in the DRC, monitoring, evaluation, and lessons learned from the field have played a significant role in the development of new activities and the refining of existing ones.

Based on analysis of trends over time in reported VAWG incidents, the IRC learned that VAWG survivors in the DRC were more likely to report a wider range of incidents, and in a shorter time period following the incident, when they could talk to someone in a local women's community-based organisation (CBO), rather than to an NGO that was perceived as 'external'. With this information, the IRC in the DRC changed its programming strategy to ensure that VAWG services were available from CBOs, with positive results that likely better reflect the reality of the types of violence that women and girls face on a day-to-day basis.

Similarly, analysis of regular monitoring tools of the IRC's activities in the DRC, along with feedback coming from clients and service providers, indicated that some VAWG survivors had severe trauma symptoms, and needed a more specialised approach than case management. Based on this identified need, the IRC partnered with mental health specialists to test a specialised mental health therapy for survivors with high and persistent trauma symptoms. An impact evaluation of this therapy showed dramatic reductions in depression, anxiety, and trauma symptoms (Bass 2013). While many service-based VAWG programmes in the DRC focus on clinical care and provision of post-exposure prophylaxis[2] for sexual violence survivors, contextualised programme data helped IRC add another important element – specialised mental health therapy – to the services already offered, in order to better meet survivors' needs.

By regularly collecting and analysing data from reported VAWG cases, and by holding discussions with staff and partners on the ground to provide context, the above are examples of how the IRC used monitoring and evaluation of programme data and lessons learned to influence programming in the DRC, leading to better practices and policies that will help prevent and protect from VAWG.

How can I know who needs VAWG services and where?

In order to provide essential, potentially life-saving services to VAWG survivors, it is crucial that VAWG services be as widely available as possible. Global studies tell us that upwards of one in three women will be raped or abused in their lifetime (World Health Organization 2013, 20). In the DRC, prevalence estimates are as high as 71 per cent of women experiencing some type of VAWG in their lifetimes (Ministry of Planning, Democratic Republic of Congo 2008, 306). While there may never be exact numbers on VAWG incidents, it is safe to say that no community is VAWG-free, so precise incidence data in a particular area should not be a prerequisite to service provision. Often, a mapping of existing VAWG services – and where they are not available – is a good guide to determine where new services are needed.

Another way to explore who needs services, and where, is to ask who is not accessing existing services. Reported VAWG data are available because there are VAWG services available, but at the same time, it can provide information on what barriers may exist to accessing these existing services. What is the profile of survivors reporting these incidents? Are they mostly adults, meaning that there may be barriers for children and adolescents to access services? Are they only reporting VAWG perpetrated by strangers, meaning that they are not reporting incidents perpetrated by intimate partners, family members, friends, and community members? Are the services available for these individuals who are not reporting, and if so, how can we increase their access to these services? This kind of analysis can ensure that existing VAWG programmes are improved and reach more VAWG survivors.

Does an increase in the reported number of cases mean there is an overall increase in the prevalence of VAWG?

Any organisation or donor involved in VAWG response and prevention would like to see a decrease in the incidence of VAWG over time. However, given that reducing VAWG requires deep-rooted attitudinal and behavioural change, this will not happen overnight.

When the number or profile of VAWG survivors reporting cases changes, it is easy to try to attribute this to a change in the frequency or types of VAWG happening in the community. This may be the case in some humanitarian settings, when significant change in the environment or context (such as a natural disaster, mass displacement, or conflict) disrupts normal social structures, and puts people at greater risk of violence. Changes in the number of reported cases of VAWG could also signify a change in the availability of services: greater or fewer services available, more or less information on the VAWG services available, or improving or deteriorating quality of services. Analysis of the context of this data, through in-depth discussions with implementing staff or other actors, can help explain any trends in changes of reported cases.

Dispelling myths: how VAWG data in the DRC are misinterpreted

Data on VAWG in the DRC have been highly visible in the media, and too often reduced to sensationalist and oversimplified sound bites, without the nuancing and detail that is needed to understand the true nature of the violence that women and girls face on a day-to-day basis. Without this contextual information, VAWG data coming out of the DRC are often misunderstood and misinterpreted, which in turn influences the kinds of programmes funded and services provided. These risk failing to respond to the real interests and needs of women and girls.

However, the use of monitoring, evaluation, and learning data from programmes and service provision offers a feasible solution to this problem, and can help implementers understand the reality of VAWG in the DRC, to dispel myths propagated in the media, to tailor services to meet women and girls' needs, and to advocate to donors and stakeholders to support these services.

Below are several common misinterpretations of VAWG data from the DRC, followed by insights and lessons learned from the IRC's ten years of programming in eastern DRC.

Myth: *The total number of VAWG incidents reported is inflated by multiple reporting and recording of each incident, since many VAWG survivors access more than one VAWG service*

The fact that a survivor is accessing more than one type of service is actually a very positive sign of different essential services being available to meet the varied needs of survivors, and that there is a functioning referral system between these service providers. It is very important to keep in mind that a survivor can have multiple needs, including medical care, psychosocial counselling, legal counselling, and economic and social support to enable her to rebuild her life and integrate into society.

Similarly, it is not unusual in one community to see many survivors reporting to one type of available service (e.g. psychosocial counselling) but not another (e.g. legal assistance). A difference in the numbers reported to each of these service providers is not a sign of inconsistency in the reported number of VAWG incidents: it is simply an indication that VAWG survivors have differing needs, and/or that the level of access to these services may differ (e.g. some services may be more costly, or less confidential). The difference in the sensitivity, urgency, or difficulty in accessing one kind of service compared to another in fact means that it is normal, and indeed expected, that survivors will access certain services more than others.

Between January and December 2013, nearly 2,000 VAWG survivors received relevant services through the IRC. Of these, 99 per cent received psychosocial services, 49 per cent received medical care, and 4 per cent received legal services. Overall, about 50 per cent of survivors received more than one service in 2013.

Additionally, double-counting can be prevented. With the current GBVIMS system, each incident of violence is given a unique code when the incident is reported and recorded. This code is used between service providers within a solid referral system to make sure that the incident is only counted once under total beneficiaries when data are compiled. The IRC's experience in the DRC demonstrates that a harmonised data management system can avoid, or at least greatly reduce, double-counting.

Myth: *VAWG service providers are hiding behind the principle of 'confidentiality', which allows them to inflate VAWG numbers or to jealously guard the survivors as 'theirs'*

> Many organizations are reluctant to share data in view of organizational competition, what respondents refer to as the 'appropriation of victims'. This means that agencies do not want to give names of victims out of fear that other organizations will approach them to become their client. As a result, duplication of names in different data bases cannot be filtered out. (Douma and Hilhorst 2012, 28)

Douma and Hilhorst's view of sharing VAWG survivors' personal identifying information is an example of misunderstanding the ethical principles behind the ways in which sensitive data should be handled and shared, or protected.

Confidentiality of VAWG survivors at all times is a core principle for VAWG service providers globally, and is a key recommendations of the World Health Organization's *Ethical and Safety Recommendations for Researching, Documenting and Monitoring Sexual Violence in Emergencies* (World Health Organization 2007). Any VAWG service provider who shared names of survivors without their consent would be breaching ethical principles.

In a context like the DRC, both VAWG survivors and service providers also face real security risks if information on specific incidents is leaked. Statements that imply that confidentiality should not be a priority for VAWG service providers are both ignoring international guidelines and demonstrating a lack of knowledge of the DRC context. At the same time, thanks to ethical VAWG data collection systems like the GBVIMS, compiled VAWG data with no identifying information about survivors can be safely shared externally.

Myth: women 'fake' being a VAWG survivor to get free services

There is no solid evidence of a multitude of 'fake' survivors reporting to VAWG service providers. Because of the nature of VAWG and the services offered, the problem of 'faking' is less likely to occur with VAWG programmes than other aid programmes, where services are less sensitive and likely more applicable to a broader population. One reason for this is that the trauma of actually reporting VAWG incidents should not be underestimated. In addition to the general trauma that all would experience, there is an additional trauma in any context in which VAWG survivors reporting for services face potential stigmatisation and insecurity (Kelly *et al.* 2011). Previous research, as well as consistent qualitative evidence from the IRC's experience in service provision, indicates the reality and severity of communities stigmatising rape survivors in Eastern Congo, and of families or spouses that abandon them (Kelly *et al.* 2011).

Survivors accessing specialised services face risks to their livelihoods, reputation, and well-being. While some actors insist that the extreme needs of populations in the DRC mean that concerns about stigma and insecurity are not sufficient to outweigh the potential benefits of accessing services, the IRC's experience does not support this – women in the DRC are just as concerned about their dignity and well-being as those anywhere else in the world, and the IRC regularly supports women and girls who delay coming forward to seek help because of these concerns. Additionally, many VAWG services are of a specialised nature, which in most cases are not relevant to those who have not experienced violence, or in the case of clinical care, invasive and uncomfortable procedures.

These and other disincentives discourage the great majority of survivors from reporting VAWG incidents at all, let alone report an incident multiple times to multiple service providers.

That said, it remains important not to create negative incentives by making services only available for survivors of sexual violence, when these are also sorely needed by others in the same communities. The case of fistula repair has been the subject of criticism for registering 'fake' survivors, in order to provide this medical service to women who need it who have not been the victims of violence; if these services are not made contingent upon experiencing sexual violence but are instead available more widely to those who need them, the accusation of creating 'fake' survivors can be avoided.

Lastly, it is important to recognise that a survivor is often accused of 'faking' her report of sexual violence if she later chooses to retract her statement to the police, or to stop pursuing legal action. In this case, community members, the police, and service providers often assume that the survivor has decided not to pursue a false allegation. However, the IRC's experience demonstrates that the truth is in fact the opposite: in many cases the pressure that communities, perpetrators, and their families place on survivors is so significant that survivors become afraid of pursuing legal proceedings, and instead are forced to say that they made up the accusation.

Myth: VAWG incidents that occur in the DRC are primarily conflict-related sexual violence

DRC has been labelled 'the rape capital of the world', an epithet that is repeated over and over in the media, usually accompanied by a photojournalistic image of a Congolese man in army fatigues with a gun slung across his shoulders. This common representation of the DRC over the past several years has a significant influence on funding streams and the types of programmes and services that are available, where they are available, and to whom.

Monitoring data from the IRC's information management system for reported VAWG cases offers a more nuanced story of perpetrators of violence. Throughout 2013, the IRC provided services to nearly 2,000 VAWG survivors in North and South Kivu in a context of frequent insecurity and population displacement, some of which was caused by confrontations between the Congolese national army and the rebel group M23.[3] Of cases reported to the IRC, 33 per cent were allegedly perpetrated by a member of an armed group, showing that conflict-related violence is indeed a very real and serious problem. However, 20 per cent of VAWG cases reported to the IRC in 2013 were perpetrated by an intimate partner, and about 18 per cent perpetrated by someone else with an everyday relationship with the survivor – family members, neighbours, teachers, and other members of the community. This means that about 38 per cent of reported VAWG cases were perpetrated by someone known to the survivor (Figure 7.2).

The IRC's programming data also tell a different story about the types of VAWG that women and girls face. Although the dominant narrative propagated in the media is the occurrence of widespread sexual violence, monitoring data from IRC programmes again provides a much more nuanced understanding.

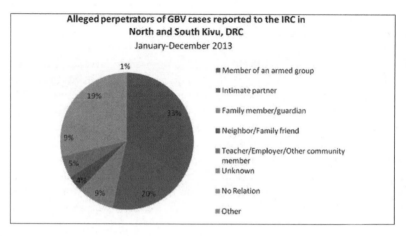

Figure 7.2 Alleged perpetrators of VAWG cases reported to the IRC in North and South Kivu, DRC –January–December 2013

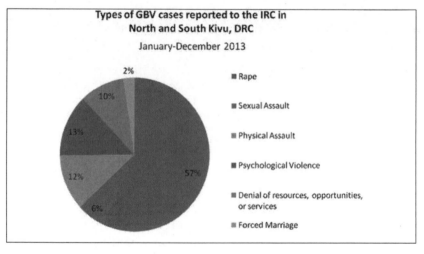

Figure 7.3 Types of VAWG cases reported to the IRC in North and South Kivu, DRC – January–December 2013

In North and South Kivu in 2013, 63 per cent of reported VAWG cases were sexual violence (rape or sexual assault). Similar to the programme data on alleged perpetrators, this confirms that sexual violence is a serious issue in eastern DRC. However, it also means that 37 per cent of reported cases were cases of physical or psychological violence, denial of resources, or forced marriage (Figure 7.3).

The IRC's programming experience in eastern DRC has also shown that survivors' decisions to report incidents of VAWG vary depending on the types of services available, and that when services focus on conflict-related sexual violence, that is the type of violence that is more frequently reported, leaving other types of violence under-reported and those survivors without services.

At the end of 2012 and beginning of 2013, as a means to better meet the needs of VAWG survivors and invest in more sustainable strategy for service provision, the IRC transitioned from partnering with local NGOs that focused more heavily on services for survivors of sexual violence, to partnering with grassroots women's CBOs that are more in touch with the needs of women and girls in their own communities. Within one year of this transition, the percentage of cases of intimate partner violence reported to IRC partners doubled, the percentage of cases of VAWG perpetrated by a family member increased by 50 per cent, and the percentage of non-sexual VAWG cases increased by 75 per cent. Since the prevailing context has not altered dramatically, the assumption can be made that it is not the kinds of violence that have changed, but rather how easily survivors of those kinds can access the services they need.

Conclusions

Monitoring, evaluation, and lessons learned from VAWG programme data are an invaluable resource for implementers, donors, and stakeholders, to make sure that life-saving VAWG services are available, appropriate, and meet the needs of survivors. These are tools that are accessible over time, and can assist in identifying programming gaps and opportunities. Implementers and stakeholders can also use programme and services data to understand the reality of women and girls, and change the international perspective to reflect these realities.

There are, of course, limits to programme data. It cannot give an idea of incidence and prevalence of VAWG overall, and changes in the number of cases reported should be understood in the specific context of service provision. However, exact numbers should not be a prerequisite for high-quality services to meet the needs of survivors. We know that VAWG happens all over the world, and we know that it happens in the DRC.

In the DRC, programming data can give us the contextual nuances that tell us that the 'conflict-related sexual violence' narrative is oversimplified. It can be combined with prevalence studies or other VAWG data to complete the picture of what is really happening in DRC. Service providers and funders should look at interventions that address other types of VAWG besides sexual violence, and ensure that their services are appropriate for survivors of violence at the hands of someone close to them, such as an intimate partner.

Some of the IRC's most successful and innovative evidence-based programmes in the DRC are inspired from analysing contextualised VAWG data from service provision and listening when women and girls voice their own interests and needs.

Acknowledgments

The authors would like to thank Kristy Crabtree for assistance with graphics and Aisha Bain for assistance on advocacy efforts.

Notes

1. Violence against women and girls (VAWG) is defined as any act of gender-based violence that results in, or is likely to result in, physical, sexual, or mental harm or suffering to women, including threats of such acts, coercion, or arbitrary deprivation of liberty, whether occurring in public or in private life. It includes a wide range of abuses occurring in the family and in the general community, including battering, sexual abuse of children, dowry-related violence, rape, female genital mutilation and other traditional practices harmful to women, non-spousal violence, and violence related to exploitation, sexual harassment and intimidation at work, in educational institutions and elsewhere, trafficking in women, forced prostitution, and violence perpetrated or condoned by the state (United Nations General Assembly 1993). Violence against women is often used as a means of perpetuating female subordination.

2. Post-exposure prophylaxis – the administering of drugs to reduce the possibility of HIV infection – is part of essential clinical post-rape care.

3. The M23 armed group consists of soldiers who participated in a mutiny from the Congolese national army in April and May 2012 and remained in control over territories in North Kivu until November 2013. The group's senior commanders have a known history of serious abuses against civilians (Human Rights Watch, http://www.hrw.org/news/2012/09/11/dr-congo-m23-rebels-committing-war-crimes, last checked by the authors April 2014).

References

Bass, Judith, Jeannie Annan, Sarah McIvor Murray, Debra Kaysen, Shelly Griffiths, Talita Cetinoglu, Karin Wachter, Laura K. Murray, and Paul Bolton (2013) 'Controlled trial of psychotherapy for Congolese survivors of sexual violence', *New England Journal of Medicine* 368(23): 2182–91.

Douma, Nynke and Dorothea Hilhorst (2012) Fonds de Commerce? Sexual violence assistance in the Democratic Republic of Congo, *Disaster Studies Occasional Paper*, Wageningen: Wageningen University.

Inter-Agency Standing Committee (2005) *Guidelines for Gender-based Violence Interventions in Humanitarian Settings*, http://www.unhcr.org/453492294.html (last checked by the authors May 2014).

Johnson, Kirsten, Jennifer Scott, Bigy Rughita, Michael Kisielewski, Jana Asher, Ricardo Ong, and Lyn Lawry (2010) 'Association of sexual violence and human rights violations with physical and mental health in territories of the Eastern Democratic Republic of Congo', *JAMA* 304(5): 553–62.

Kelly, Jocelyn, Theresa Betancourt, Denis Mukwege, Robert Lipton, and Michael J. VanRooyen (2011) 'Experiences of female survivors of sexual violence in eastern Democratic Republic of the Congo: a mixed-methods study', *Conflict and Health* 5(25): 2–8.

Ministry of Planning, Democratic Republic of Congo (2008) *Demographic and Health Survey 2007*, Calverton, MD: Macro International Inc.

Palermo, Tia, Jennifer Bleck, and Amber Peterman (2013) 'Tip of the iceberg: reporting and gender-based violence in developing countries',

American Journal of Epidemiology, http://aje.oxfordjournals.org/content/early/2013/12/12/aje.kwt295.abstract (last checked by the authors May 2014).

Peterman, Amber, Tia Palermo, and Caryn Bredenkamp (2011) 'Estimates and determinants of sexual violence against women in the Democratic Republic of Congo', *American Journal of Public Health* 101(6): 1060–67.

United Nations General Assembly (1993) 48/104: *Declaration on the Elimination of Violence against Women* (A/RES/48/104), New York: United Nations.

U.S. Government Accountability Office (2011) *Information on the Rate of Sexual Violence in War-Torn Eastern DRC and Adjoining Countries*, http://www.gao.gov/assets/330/320957.pdf (last checked by the authors May 2014).

World Health Organization (2007) *Ethical and Safety Recommendations for Researching, Documenting and Monitoring Sexual Violence in Emergencies*, http://www.who.int/gender/documents/OMS_Ethics&Safety10Aug07.pdf (last checked by the authors May 2014).

World Health Organization (2013) *Global and Regional Estimates of Violence against Women: Prevalence and Health Effects of Intimate Partner Violence and Non-partner Sexual Violence*, http://genderviolence.lshtm.ac.uk/files/VAW-report-AFTER-EMBARGOED-complete-document.pdf (last checked by the authors May 2014).

About the authors

Marie-France Guimond is a Research Specialist for the International Rescue Committee's Research, Evaluation and Learning Unit based in New York. Postal address: 122 E 42nd Street, New York, NY 10168-1289, USA. Email: MarieFrance.Guimond@rescue.org

Katie Robinette is the Monitoring, Evaluation & Research Coordinator for the International Rescue Committee's Women's Protection and Empowerment Program in the Democratic Republic of the Congo. Postal address: 122 E 42nd Street, New York, NY 10168-1289, USA. Email: Katie.Robinette@rescue.org

CHAPTER 8

Learning about women's empowerment in the context of development projects: do the figures tell us enough?

Jane Carter, Sarah Byrne, Kai Schrader, Humayun Kabir, Zenebe Bashaw Uraguchi, Bhanu Pandit, Badri Manandhar, Merita Barileva, Norbert Pijls and Pascal Fendrich

Abstract

In this chapter, we consider three projects implemented by Helvetas Swiss Intercooperation: a project in Nepal focusing on capacity building (vocational skills training); a project in Bangladesh focusing on income generation; and a project in Kosovo working on agency – enhancing the voice of citizens in local governance. The chapter examines how donor requirements for demonstrating evidence-based results challenge project management in different ways, how facts and figures are generated, how experience is translated into reports, and how qualitative methods are used for evaluations. This is compared against a stakeholder (participant) perspective of their degree of satisfaction with project performance, obtained through case studies or focus group discussions. We take the four dimensions of empowerment, notably 'power-over', 'power-to', 'power-within', and 'power-with', and consider the degree to which these are captured through qualitative and quantitative monitoring and evaluation systems. The main finding is that quantitative methods stress aspects of 'power-to', whilst qualitative methods have potential to provide insights into a broader range of outcomes and impacts.

Key words: women's empowerment, monitoring and evaluation, agency, social change

Introduction

Monitoring and evaluation (M&E) can be potentially a powerful tool for awareness-raising, knowledge-sharing, and empowerment itself. In this paper we consider the M&E systems of three different development projects implemented by our organisation, HELVETAS Swiss Intercooperation (henceforward Helvetas), and examine how these support women's empowerment in contexts of gender inequality. We reflect on how these different development

http://dx.doi.org/10.3362/9781780447049.008

interventions approach women's empowerment through three ways, each specific to one project: supporting women to build their personal endowments (capacities); enhance their economic assets (income); and promote their voice, or agency (Kabeer 1999).

It is widely accepted that development projects focusing on power, and on increasing participation in decision-making, have greater difficulty in fulfilling conventional donor M&E requirements which emphasise countable inputs and outputs. We recognise that women's empowerment is challenging to measure because the empowerment process is not directly observable, and needs to be described through proxy indicators, indirect measures, or signs. Empowerment is a multi-dimensional process which is related in a vast number of ways to many factors, rendering perception and subjectivities (Kabeer 1998) as well as context extremely important (Mahmud *et al.* 2012). Furthermore, empowerment processes are interwoven with relational aspects, an examination of which can be essential for 'understanding resistances, successes, re-negotiations and unintended outcomes of women's empowerment initiatives' (Fenneke Reysoo, personal communication, 24 April 2014). Yet we are limited in what we can cover here.

In this chapter, therefore, we will set out to explore – from the point of development practitioners – how we learn, as development practitioners, about women's empowerment and, more specifically, how we monitor and evaluate the outcomes of different project interventions aiming to empower women. The chapter starts with a description of three projects we are using here as case studies, their activities in support of women's empowerment, and their M&E systems. We then consider whether or not empowerment as an aim has in fact been 'lost in translation' because of the systems we use. Our findings show that understanding empowerment requires mixed methods, that capturing empowerment as a holistic process requires equally holistic M&E systems capable of analysing all power's dimensions ('power-over', 'power-to', 'power-within', and 'power-with'), and that we should design the M&E of women's empowerment to be itself an empowering, voice-enhancing, process. With this chapter, we aim to generate wider reflection and debate among our colleagues in our own organisation and in the wider development community on how, in a context of increasing demand in development circles for results expressed in figures, development practitioners can capture important changes in women's lives.

Learning about empowerment: points of departure and conceptual framing

This chapter adopts an approach that may differ from that of many readers, whom we assume to be gender specialists focusing on women's empowerment issues. A natural aim in this case would be to attempt to capture change in a manner that is carefully honed to the particular empowerment processes at play. Instead, as development practitioners engaged in supporting the implementation of development projects in a variety of ways, we felt it interesting to consider the regular, mainly quantitative M&E methods and results used, and to examine how – indeed whether – they provide insight into complex processes of change in gender power relations.

Project M&E systems are generally required to serve three main functions: accountability, steering, and learning. Accountability tends to be upward, to the donor, but can potentially also be downward, to the end users or 'beneficiaries' (e.g. through public or social audit, or beneficiary assessment[1]). M&E data are also used for the future steering of projects – that is, responding to social and other context changes, both planned and unplanned, to ensure that the intervention remains on course and relevant to the interests and needs of the targeted population. Steering requires sound knowledge of the possible final impact of the project in the given context. In this chapter we set out to examine the 'fit' between the types of data that are collected for the purposes of accountability, steering, and learning, and women's realities on the ground.

Donor demands for quantitative evidence are currently increasing, since figures can be framed as 'value for money' in ways that facts and anecdotal evidence gleaned from qualitative data cannot (Eyben *et al.* 2013). Feminist critiques of the limitations of quantitative data for capturing complex change have existed for many years (an example is Jayaratne and Stewart 1991). Such critiques question who has the power to 'know' what, and how power comes into the process of producing knowledge. These critiques can be applied to a wide range of practices involved in conceptualising and implementing M&E systems, for example in the selection of indicators. As Caroline Moser (2007) points out, by choosing what to measure, the policymaker, advocate, researcher, or development practitioner can choose the story she or he wants to tell. However, the stories we tell are not at all, or only partially, our own stories. Hence the point of departure for us as we set out to write this chapter was, how do the stories of change that we tell relate to those that our 'primary stakeholders' tell?

As we wrote the chapter, we compared the information gained from M&E systems against the way that individual women who have benefited from the three projects described their experiences. In doing this, we sought to understand more about the processes through which changes in individuals' life experiences are translated into M&E data and, in turn, into information of various kinds. Ultimately, we need this better understanding to ensure that institutional learning takes place, and to be confident that we know all we need to know to ensure projects and their M&E systems genuinely support the empowerment of women.

The case study projects and process of analysis

The projects we focused on for this chapter are the Employment Fund (EF) in Nepal, Samriddhi in Bangladesh, and LOGOS in Kosovo. The EF provides vocational training/skills development and facilitates access to employment for young people, the Samriddhi project fosters employment and income generation through selected value chains, whilst LOGOS promotes effective, participatory, and socially inclusive local governance. The projects' key characteristics are outlined in Table 8.1. Each is executed by Helvetas, and funded in all or in part by the Swiss Agency for Development Cooperation (SDC), meaning that reporting requirements and processes are broadly similar. Each has a quite comprehensive M&E system in place.

In gathering material for this study, those authors directly responsible for project management and/or M&E first completed a standardised questionnaire (devised by the principal authors) about their project's approach to women's empowerment, the M&E system design and operation, and the requirements of the different users of the information gathered. We shared and reflected on these answers. As a second line of enquiry, each project provided feedback from some of the women implicated in their activities – collected in two cases from a focus group discussion, and in one case (EF) from some previously elaborated individual case studies.

The country settings of the three projects are, of course, very different. Nepal, still in political turmoil after its civil war, is gradually addressing the deep discrimination experienced by women, so-called low castes (especially Dalits), and Janajati (indigenous) groups, as perpetuated under the Hindu caste system (Bennett 2006). One effect of the post-1990 democratisation process (and Maoist movement)[2] was to raise social consciousness, questioning discrimination on the basis of caste and gender, but it nevertheless still remains common in rural areas (Sharma and Donini 2010). Bangladesh has taken many strides to further the position of women since gaining independence just over 40 years ago. The schooling of girl children is often claimed as a particular success. Yet it remains a strongly patriarchal country characterised by stark gender inequalities (Mahmud et al. 2012). Kosovo, the youngest and smallest country of the three, is still in the process of institutional state building. The effects of communism, conflict, and everyday life in a difficult socio-economic context have had contradictory outcomes on gender relations and the role of women in society (Jafa 2002). The recent visceral war has left deep trauma, and the still on-going effects of the very high levels of violence against women during the war are rarely publicly discussed (UNFPA 2005).

Overview of project activities in relation to women's empowerment

Although the three projects were chosen for the different thematic focus that they have each adopted in supporting women's empowerment, in reality the 'specialist focus' is not exclusive, and there is a degree of thematic overlap. Furthermore, whilst all three projects make a particular attempt to reach women, they do so from a perspective of promoting inclusivity, actively bringing women into the development process rather than simply assuming their participation. It is recognised that unless women are deliberately targeted, they are less likely than men to participate in the activities on offer (in the case of the EF in Nepal, the same principle is applied to members of discriminated castes). At the same time, none of the projects focus exclusively on women.

Table 8.1 Key fatures of the three 'case study' projects.

	Employment Fund (EF)	Samriddhi	LOGOS
Where	Nepal	Bangladesh	Kosovo
What	Improve the living conditions of economically and socially disadvantaged youth providing *occupational skills training* and ensure their gainful employment through private-sector Training and Employment Service Providers (T&Es)	Contribute to the sustainable well-being and resilience of poor and extreme poor men and women in selected areas of Northern Bangladesh through economic empowerment by participating in selected value chains	Selected *partner municipalities* in South-Eastern Kosovo *are more accountable*, transparent, equitable, and effective in local governance and able to deliver key services to satisfy all citizen groups
Start	(2008–) 2011–2013 (–2015)	2010–2013 (–2014)	(2007–) 2010–2012 (–2013)
Funding	SDC/UKaid/World Bank	SDC	SDC
Budget (million US$)	6–7 per year	2.3 per year	4.7 (divided by 3 years)
Primary stakeholders[a]	Economically poor and socially discriminated youth in Nepal (12–15,000 youths per annum)	Poor and extreme poor men and women in selected areas of Northern Bangladesh – with a special focus on women since mid-2010	Citizens of nine selected partner municipalities in South-Eastern Kosovo
Implementing agency	Helvetas and EF Secretariat[b]	Helvetas and 18 NGOs, 62 SPA,[c] 100 companies and trading entities	Helvetas and partner municipalities
M&E systems: main common characteristics	All three projects: • Gather regularly data on activities, spending, and outputs disaggregated by gender. • Undergo external evaluations, usually using DAC criteria.[d] • Have a complex set-up of M&E methods and tools providing quantitative and qualitative data. • Provide quantitative data to donors, Helvetas Head Offices and implementing partners (surveys, audit).		

M&E systems: specific/distinctive characteristics	• Complement information with qualitative data collected through (systematic) direct observation, semi-structured interviews, focus group discussion, and case studies. • Regularly (bi-annual and annual) report to donors (accountability) and also use M&E results for adjusting project's activities (steering) and learning.		
	Over 60% of staff involved in results and process monitoring. Partner organisations monitor own performance and outcome; project verifies through random sampling	Individual service providers and partner organisations gather output and outcome data. Specific Monitoring and Results Measurement (MRM) Team	Monitoring of outcome is outsourced: annual citizen satisfaction survey undertaken by a private consultancy firm
	Tracer studies, impact assessment	Value chains and market analysis	Complementary SDC project on the 'demand side'
	Employment Fund (EF)	Samriddhi	LOGOS
	Dissemination through reports, presentations, publications, Web, videos, newspapers, radio and TV. Online database accessible to implementing partners and project staff	Dissemination through reports, publications, documentary videos, newsletter, website	Dissemination through reports and presentations to donors, Helvetas, and partner municipalities
M&E periodicity	Intensive five stages usually within one year	Six-monthly	Annual and six-monthly
M&E unit	Individuals	Households and producers belonging to producer groups	Municipalities

ªWe prefer the term 'primary stakeholder' to 'beneficiary', as it avoids any 'top-down' connotation, and upholds the sense of those benefiting from the project activities as right holders, not passive recipients. However, we are conscious that 'primary stakeholder' can be misconstrued to mean local implementing agencies, which is not our meaning. To avoid any confusion, we sometimes revert in this chapter to the word 'beneficiary'.

ᵇThe Employment Fund Secretariat is the official body managing the Employment Fund; further details may be found at www.employmentfund.org.np/ or http://epal.helvetas. org/en/our_projects/employment_fund.cfm.

ᶜService providers in this context are individual men and women who have particular skills in horticulture, animal husbandry, financial management, or similar matters, and who offer their services on a remunerative basis. They have voluntarily joined associations of individuals with similar skills to facilitate access to information and physical inputs (such as pesticides, veterinary medicines, etc.). Most Service Provider Associations (SPAs) are of mixed gender, but their leadership is almost always men.

ᵈThe Development Assistance Committee of the Organisation for Economic Co-operation and Development (OECD-DAC) establishes five minimum criteria for evaluating development intervention that should be considered: relevance, effectiveness, efficiency, impact, and sustainability (www.oecd.org/dac/evaluation/daccriteriaforevaluatingdevelopmentassistance.htm).

Ways in which women are pro-actively brought into the project activities are varied; a brief (although not complete) overview is provided here.

The EF project in Nepal operates a 'carrot and stick' incentive scheme with the private vocational training institutions whom it partners. These service providers receive payments for each participant they train. 'Carrots' include a higher payment by the project to the institutions for women trainee participants than men (and also for Dalit or Janajati trainees) who complete training satisfactorily and are in gainful employment six months afterwards. Another effective 'carrot' exists in the form of less strict criteria for accepting women candidates than men (such as lower educational qualifications, given that girls often have to drop out of school to attend to family commitments). Since it is not always easy for training providers to recruit women candidates, this serves to facilitate selection. The training of Dalit women, traditionally doubly discriminated, attracts a premium for the institutes. 'Sticks' include fixed targets (60 per cent) for the proportion of women trained. If an institute trains a higher proportion of men than it is contracted to, it is simply not paid for these additional male trainees.

Samriddhi in Bangladesh builds on a history of previous development projects that included activities such as training local women as female mentors who conduct participatory gender analyses, and facilitate follow-up activities, within the communities in which they live. The post-2009 project has focused on specific 'value chains' (that is, the range of different businesses within the process of production and transformation through to sale of the processed products), promoting ways in which poor people can gain the greatest benefit. This was initially done without specific consideration of gender dynamics. Unfortunately, but not really surprisingly, the value chains with the greatest 'added value' potential (that is, the highest profit for producers or primary processors) turned out to be those dominated by men (e.g. bullock fattening for beef, and fish and fruit production). Facilitating women's involvement in such value chains was generally not possible due to strict gender-defined roles,[3] so since mid-2010, there has been a deliberate effort on the part of the project to focus on value chains dominated by women (such as medicinal plants, cotton crafts, and backyard poultry). In addition, local women as well as men have been encouraged to become private service providers, and thus gain an income through the sale of their knowledge and skills.

In promoting transparent, accountable, and inclusive local governance in Kosovo, LOGOS uses the tool of gender-responsive budgeting.[4] Thus, a clear spotlight is placed on the implications for men and women in the allocation of municipal funds, the planning and monitoring of which is conducted in a participatory process (Kroesschell 2012). All citizens – including women and members of minority communities – are actively encouraged to attend and participate in meetings discussing budgetary allocations. Furthermore, through institutionalising the scrutiny of budgets according to their impact on men and women, LOGOS supports women to advance their views both individually and collectively, ensuring that their voice has an impact on local government actions. The project also supports publicity campaigns on gender equality to raise awareness. To reinforce the gender-responsive budgeting process, it has ensured that municipal gender officers have a dedicated budget, enabling them to have an impact in their roles. In many countries it has been noted that government officials focusing on gender and women's issues often lack the economic resources to be effective in their roles, so a specific budget is potentially empowering for them. However, it should perhaps be noted that LOGOS differs from the other two projects in that the emphasis is on supporting the state institutional framework (working with the 'duty bearers', in governance terms). This means that the immediate beneficiaries are the municipal staff, rather than women and men citizens themselves.

All the projects have identified, and seek to address, a variety of specific challenges faced by women that potentially hinder them from involvement in project activities. In summary, the main challenges common to all three projects are:

- *Child care*: both the EF and Samriddhi try to ensure that child-care arrangements are in place if needed by women participants, although both also recognise that this is a complicated issue that cannot necessarily be addressed by simply ensuring a safe, supervised space for young children. In recognition of the fact that women in rural areas commonly have children in their teens or early 20s and are thus generally not free to absent themselves for training in institutions based some distance from their homes, the EF maintains a higher upper age limit (but the same lower limit of age 16) for accepting women rather than men. This means that project-supported training opportunities are still open to them in their late 20s or early 30s – also giving time to gain the approval of sometimes sceptical mothers-in-law – whilst for men the age limit is 25.
- *Female staff and role models*: in all three countries, gender-sensitive men and women, are required on the staff of the projects. Women approach other women more readily, whilst gender-sensitive men can provide excellent role models; the importance of the input of both sexes is underlined in our organisational human resources policy. Thus, it is important to have women as well as men in the roles of trainers, service providers, municipal officers, and so on. Our experience is that this is not always easy to arrange, but is at least actively sought.
- *Finances*: in both Nepal and Bangladesh, the projects facilitate access to credit for women involved in project activities. In Kosovo, the fact that the project provides a budget for municipal gender officers has given them a power in decision-making that they did not have before, and an opportunity to show that carefully planned gender-responsive interventions really make a difference. This can be seen from the quotation below, from Shefkije Mehmeti, head of municipal assembly from Novoberde municipality:

> *Starting from 2012, the municipality has allocated a budget for the gender officer based on the action plan that was developed in co-operation with*

> *LOGOS. The change was very big in ourselves because our self-confidence has increased as for the first time we felt even as women we could manage our own funds.* (Focus Group Discussion organised by LOGOS, 12 December 2013)

- *Women-focused training*: beyond the training offered to all project participants, the EF, Samriddhi, and LOGOS all offer some training courses only for women. These are specifically targeted to women's needs in business training in Samriddhi and EF (e.g. how to develop a business plan, how to access credit, taking into account the obstacles faced by women in so doing); 'life skill training' (EF); and legal rights, health, and violence against women (LOGOS).
- *Promotion of non-stereotypical roles*: this is particularly done by the EF, which offers counselling and financial incentives to women willing to take up male-dominated trades such as carpentry, masonry and mechanics.

As already noted, all three projects have quite sophisticated and comprehensive M&E systems in place, as briefly outlined in the project summary table (Table 8.1). The next section gives an overview of some of the points which we consider to be the most interesting and significant.

M&E systems used by the projects: an overview

Like most other donors, SDC requires M&E systems that provide at minimum information for the tracking of spending (focusing, for example, on activities and inputs) and outputs (for example, the number of participants in the project, the volume of products marketed, or the number of jobs obtained after participation). It is usually mandatory for projects supported by SDC to use a logical framework[5] (and it certainly was in our three cases). Logical frameworks have indicators that are grouped into output, outcome, and impact level. There is also the expectation that baseline data have been established at the start of the project, against which the values for the indicators can be compared over the years. In practice, this is not always as easy as it sounds – thus, for example, the EF relies mainly on self-assessment by the people whom the project involves and aims to benefit (we use the term 'primary stakeholders'), to collect its baseline data. However, this yields information which is considered less reliable than the project would like.

All three projects adhere to minimum M&E standards as defined by the OECD-DAC. In addition, each of them aims to reach topic-specific principles, criteria, and standards set for M&E. Samriddhi, notably, adheres to the DCED (Donor Committee for Enterprise Development) standard for value chains (see Kabir and Uraguchi 2013). Quantitative data are regularly (monthly, half yearly, annually, and bi-annually) gathered, fed into a database, and analysed, although the modalities vary. In the EF, for example, project staff undertake the bulk of M&E work, from data collection to analysis; indeed, over two-thirds

(70 per cent) of staff – and 54 per cent of full-time staff – are employed on M&E duties. By comparison, LOGOS employs external consultants to collect much of its M&E data, with the rationale that this avoids bias, and leaves staff free to concentrate on their advisory and facilitation tasks.

Disaggregating data by gender and other identities

All the personal information generated in the M&E systems is disaggregated by gender and (where appropriate) caste or ethnicity. This makes it possible to track trends in women's participation, and their social and economic situation – as far as this can be defined through the indicators used. Examples from EF include the number of women completing training successfully, and the number in gainful employment six months after training (categorised further by stereotypical and non-stereotypical occupations). In Samriddhi, examples include the number of women who have been involved in the project as producers and now have an increased income, and a self-reported increase in participants who are taking an active role in household decision-making. Similarly, the number of women working outside their homes as service providers is recorded. For LOGOS, the figures collected include the number of women participating actively in municipal meetings or selected as council representatives.

Using M&E information in project steering

All these kinds of information are not only needed for accountability to donors, but undoubtedly have a valuable role in project steering if used to full effect. Humayun Kabir, a Monitoring Specialist for Samriddhi, offered an example of how this link between M&E and project steering can be fostered consciously. Gender-disaggregated data are a clear requirement for the Samriddhi log-frame at many levels. This revealed that there were fewer women than men present in the local-level Service Provider Association (SPA) executive committees, and in some, none at all:

> We noticed in our monitoring that there was no woman LSP [local service provider] in the executive committee of the Badargonj [Rangpur] SPA. So we pointed this out and they acknowledged the problem and took action to include a woman. This shows how monitoring can be used to positive effect. (Personal communication during a project workshop, 2013)

In LOGOS, the normal reporting for the log-frame has been augmented by a strong emphasis on monitoring gender aspects of the project through the budgets of the project municipalities themselves. Over the past two years, all key personnel involved in LOGOS have received intensive training in the use of gender-responsive budgeting.

As a result, each municipality is now required to develop its annual budget through a participatory process that includes a clear analysis of the gender implications of financial allocations.

Integrating and using qualitative findings

Whilst figures and budgetary allocations are important, all three projects recognise that quantitative data alone are not enough to inform project steering.
Furthermore, in addition to the donor demand for hard, evidence-based facts,
more qualitative, 'human-interest' information is also welcome. Thus, tools
such as semi-structured and in-depth interviews, focus group discussions, and
case studies are employed to collect such additional material. 'Additional' is,
in most cases, the important word here, as the information gained does not
substitute the figures, but rather fleshes them out by giving additional information and meaning/interpretation. An exception is the citizens-based survey
used under LOGOS to track public satisfaction (or otherwise) with the functioning of the supported municipalities. This does offer a potential substitute
for conventional quantitative methods of data collection, collecting mainly
qualitative information using a statistically relevant sample. Conducted on
an annual basis (two in the last year of the current phase) by an external
consultancy company, these provide information regarding citizen perceptions of municipality performance in service delivery. They serve as the main
information base used to track the impact of the project on transparent and
accountable municipality functioning.

Learning and innovation through flexible systems

All three projects have a degree of flexibility in their M&E systems which
allows for learning and innovation. This is an important feature, which all
have used. The EF switched from monitoring all beneficiaries in the early days
to using a sample approach once the volume of project funding and numbers of beneficiaries grew. Samriddhi faced many challenges in adapting the
M&E system used by its predecessor projects, and had to modify it extensively.
LOGOS initially used the M&E system developed by the Ministry of Local
Government Administration. However, it proved unreliable and inadequately
gender sensitive, so LOGOS developed its own system which is now likely to
be taken up by the Ministry. LOGOS has managed to bring gender-responsive
thinking into municipality operations in a way that gives hope for up-scaling
to the national level. This illustrates another important point: projects need to
be sensitive, if relevant, to existing institutional systems, and to try to improve
and work with them if possible – or at least in compatibility with them.

Putting a price on M&E

As a final point before discussing our findings, the cost of M&E systems should
be noted. Many donors limit the total cost of M&E to around 5–7 per cent of
the total project budget, but this is difficult to stipulate, given the very different nature and significance of development projects. Furthermore, the cost
can be calculated in different ways, especially with regard to staffing costs.
The question remains: are sophisticated M&E systems themselves 'value for

money' in terms of the information that they provide – to the donor, to project staff and partners, and to the project beneficiaries?

Having given an account of some of the main features of the M&E systems in our three case-study projects, in the next section we set out some key observations with regard to the three M&E systems, focusing particularly on the measurement of women's empowerment. We highlight some of the practical implications of our findings relating to the process of data collection, the type of data collected, what is being measured and what, in turn, can be demonstrated or learned from these data.

Discussing our main findings: lost in translation?

As we stated at the beginning of this chapter, our original hypothesis was that the familiar and predominantly quantitative M&E methods we use are most useful in capturing evidence of those aspects of empowerment which deal with skills and training – capacity building – and also useful in capturing evidence relating to increases in women's economic assets. We hypothesised that these methods would be least useful in assessing change as a result of projects aiming to support women's voice. However, upon analysis, we realised that the main issue in all cases is capturing the 'soft' aspects of empowerment, as we describe further below.

Understanding empowerment processes requires mixed methods

> *Not everything that counts can be counted, and not everything that can be counted counts.* (Quote often attributed to Einstein, but which was actually William Bruce Cameron in 1963)

Clearly, all three projects on which we focus in this chapter are collecting huge amounts of quantitative data, doing so in a resource-intensive manner that involves many different people, from the 'beneficiaries', producers and service providers, to the staff of the project, specific monitoring task groups, and consultants. The EF and Samriddhi, in particular, use relatively sophisticated tools to collect, proceed, analyse, and store the large volume of quantitative data that they amass. This is keeping with the perception that such data are 'objective' and 'scientific', despite a literature which explores the biases and misconceptions that lie beneath this view (Oakley 2000). Whilst quantitative data are required by the donor – and certainly much of the data are used – it is also clear to all staff involved that quantitative data alone are inadequate to capture fully the complex and mainly qualitative nature of changes at individual, household, and social levels. All three projects need qualitative information to analyse progress further and interpret/understand changes relating to empowerment processes.

In her classic exploration of empowerment in development initiatives in Honduras, Jo Rowlands (1997, 13) distinguishes four different kinds of power:

coercive 'power-over' which reflects structural power relations in society, the 'power-to' of individual agency, which can potentially challenge structural power, 'power-within', felt by individuals as psychological strength, and 'power-with' – many individuals acting collectively. Development interventions focusing on the empowerment of women should be interested in building both the self-confidence of 'power-within' which supports power-to, and fostering opportunities for women take the collective action which is an essential part of fostering wider change to male 'power-over ' women as a social group.

M&E can capture some evidence of increased 'power-to' in numbers of people trained in a skill or knowledge, or able to market their products in a new way, or mobile phones distributed to enable women traders to share knowledge (this last example would also be an indicator which could potentially indicate increases in 'power-with'). However, 'power-within' is a realm of empowerment which does not directly lend itself to being captured by quantitative M&E methods.

Clearly, it is imperative to use mixed methods for gathering qualitative and quantitative information, if we are to understand all aspects of empowerment processes. Only then can M&E accurately reflect women's realities. While some initiatives have been taken to develop a systematic multi-method analytical approach (see Stern *et al.* 2012), this is a matter on which further reflection would be useful.

While qualitative M&E methods allow for a more nuanced description and understanding of changes, the way in which qualitative information is collected can also be criticised in tending to highlight successes rather than failures. The way in which questions are phrased (closed or open-ended) can beg a positive answer (e.g. 'What were the main things you learned?', rather than, 'Please give your views on the training'). Even if obvious, this is a common problem. Similarly, if data are gathered by persons implicated in the project, the respondents may feel a need to be polite and avoid mentioning negative aspects. Or they may, to the contrary, seek to highlight negative aspects in order to receive further contributions/input from the project. Qualitative data may also treated with suspicion, on the grounds of lacking statistical rigour and representativeness. Moreover, while any kind of data can be manipulated and used in an instrumental way to achieve goals set by project planners and implementers which are not the goals of the actual research participants themselves, qualitative data are often seen as more easily abused in this way. These criticisms can be responded to by improving the quality of M&E to ensure rigorous qualitative findings, various methods including triangulation, respondent validation, clarity on methodology, reflexivity, and attention to negative cases (Mays and Pope 2000).

Finally, whilst qualitative data are expected to add to the depth and richness of M&E, this is not automatic. If qualitative information is collected by an external agency with a clear, pre-determined mandate (as in the case of LOGOS), there is the risk that much potentially interesting information is ignored as irrelevant to the task in hand, and not transmitted to the project staff.

Understanding empowerment as holistic and moving beyond dichotomies

Our second observation concerns the need to move beyond commonly perceived dichotomies between quantitative M&E methods including closed-ended questions seen as yielding 'hard' data (e.g. numbers of individuals trained, measurable increases in income) and qualitative, open-ended methods (such as in-depth interviews) seen as yielding 'soft' data, and between ideas of empowerment as increasing agency as distinct from consciousness raising and confidence building.

Despite being characterised as yielding 'soft' data, research methods which involve open-ended discussion including focus group discussions and case studies yield a mix of 'hard' and 'soft' data. Hard data include shifts in decision-making within marriage – for example, on women's right and freedom to travel, or to choose their own clothes. Research methods associated with collecting qualitative data often actually reveal unexpected quantitative data, including changes in children's school attendance, better nutrition, and so on. However, projects do not set out to monitor such a wide range of outcomes, due to the cost of collecting mountains of data and the challenge of attribution (e.g. linking women's capacity building to children's nutritional status). In contrast, 'soft' data can be characterised as perceptions and impressions of less tangible and material changes, which nevertheless have immense significance in women's lives: for example, women's sense of increased self-confidence, and perceptions of greater respect in the community. These outcomes are actually more readily attributable to project activities, but are not yet specifically monitored.

We were struck as we explored the three projects that, as the following quotations show, and they are typical in this respect, the changes associated with 'soft' data appear to be what the women value most in projects. While this is probably a very obvious point for feminists working with women, starting from supporting the development of a sense of 'power-within', it is noteworthy for practitioners who tend to focus on supporting 'power-to' through provision of material resources and other tangible changes. In contrast, feminist models of power emphasise the connections between different kinds of power and their impact on each other.

The EF's activities to support the growth of 'power-to' via training inputs had a marked impact on one woman's sense of 'power-within' – which in turn boosted her business by extending her 'power-to'. Bimala Biswhakarma, aged 26, who attended three months of training in a particular form of weaving known as Dhaka at a technical institute in Birtamode, Jhapa, was interviewed on 28 April 2012 as one of a limited number of individual life histories gathered to complement the project's tracer study[6]. It may be noted that she grew up doubly discriminated, both for her sex, and as a Dalit. She stated:

After acquiring the skills from the training I have totally transformed my previous identity. In the past people used to know me through my husband's name and I could hardly talk with outsiders. Now equipped with my skills I can openly talk to people. And with my income I am sustaining my family.

Sarita Sijapati, aged 21, who attended three months of training in mobile phone repairs as part of the EF's activities, also gave an account of dramatic change to her sense of power and status within the community via an interview in Bhimduttanagar, Kanchanpur (8 October 2013):

> *I found the perception of society towards me is quite changed. I am also in a women's group which we formed recently and I have respect in my group. My colleagues ask me to mediate if there are any difficulties in the group. Some months ago people used to show me pity for my condition, but now they praise me for my success. This enhanced my self-respect and it also encouraged me to expand my business.*

As Lynn McIntyre *et al.* (2013, 454) have written, approaches that focus on story-telling, life histories, and other narrative methods can render visible the otherwise 'unmeasured spheres of gender (in)equality and women's (dis) empowerment'. They can also make visible changes in power relations, as in the quotation here from Bangladesh.

> *Before taking part in the project-initiated interventions, I was not allowed to visit places outside my house. This all changed after I joined the duck-rearing producers' group. My income and communication skills increased and improved. Due to the income and awareness, my husband allows me to attend different meetings of the producers' group, village, Union, Upazila, and district levels. Due to my involvement in the producers' group, other producers encouraged me to run for a local government election as member in Union Parisad* [UP – lowest tier of local government in Bangladesh]. *I was motivated to try and finally was successful in winning the election. From a simple housewife, I am now an elected member of the UP.* (Rekaha Rani, participant in Focus Group Discussion organised by Samriddhi, 22 December 2013)

Open-ended research methods which can capture a broad range of outcomes (expected and unexpected) clearly have an important role when monitoring and evaluating projects aiming to support women's empowerment. The widespread preference for quantitative data in M&E adds a new twist to this since experiences translated in quantitative terms can result in such a different report of reality compared with experiences translated into narratives which reveal perceptions and opinions.

Furthermore, if the process of translation privileges research methods which use more closed questioning methodologies, it may lose – or miss the opportunity to make visible – some significant elements of changes.

Understanding the empowerment of individuals

Gender and development literature emphasises that women's own perceptions of empowerment are both specific to them as individuals, and particular to their social and economic context. These perceptions are not necessarily shared with project staff, or with women in other social and economic contexts. Thus, the reality of 'beneficiaries' is not the same as the one of the project staff and copying successful approaches in order to standardise development interventions in 'recipes' is not viable. As Dee and Ibn Ali (2010) argue, the best way to measure empowerment is to ask those directly concerned. The more that project 'beneficiaries' have the opportunity to be actively engaged in the process of knowledge production, the more space they will have to represent reality in their own terms. But this will not necessarily be in statistically valid figures.

M&E can track many changes which occur at the individual level. In the projects we looked at, there are ways of gaining information on empowerment of women as individuals – for example, the EF tracks individuals through tracer studies. Both EF and Samriddhi plan to place more emphasis on individuals' self-identified indicators of empowerment in future. Samriddhi, up to now focusing on households, aims to orientate its M&E system to individuals in the future.

Attribution in a complex wider context of change

As a final and fourth observation, M&E systems are inevitably project-focused, yet they do not operate in a vacuum. 'Attribution or contribution?' is, of course, a perennial M&E dilemma – but it is nevertheless important to take into account the actions of other projects, the individual, and general self-development and contextual changes. The more an M&E system tries to rely on quantitative data alone for its analysis of how it has contributed to change, the more difficult this is. As a case in point, and as already mentioned, we are aware that women's economic empowerment is likely to lead to improved child nutrition, and of research in Bangladesh that shows this (Bhagowalia *et al.* 2012). However, establishing a causal link between Samriddhi and the children of women 'beneficiaries' would require a data collection system far beyond the scope and means of a development project.

Conclusions

We began this paper by noting that M&E systems are generally required to serve three main functions: accountability (both upward but also potentially downward), steering, and learning. Of these, we fear that it is upward accountability that is gaining ground. In times of economic constraint, donor agencies and implementing bodies are under heavy pressure to demonstrate 'value for money' in their activities. This is certainly the case for bilateral co-operation, budgets for which are under increasing scrutiny by politicians – and here we are thinking well beyond Switzerland, where the donor agency retains a degree (albeit shrinking) of political autonomy. Inevitably, 'value for money' seems to require quantifiable facts. Nevertheless we wonder if better communication on the part of development professionals about the worth of qualitative evidence in demonstrating value could mitigate this demand.

There is a growing body of literature advocating the use of mixed methods for M&E (see Stern *et al*. 2012, amongst others). Our own findings have shown that this would allow a much more nuanced view of outcomes in terms of women's empowerment and, importantly, would leave space for women to identify their own indicators of change. At the time of writing the conclusion to this paper, one of us was struck to read the following comment made by a woman who had participated in a training session in Kyrgyzstan, which perfectly highlights the issue we have raised in this paper:

> *Question: Would you like other farmers to join such project activities?*
>
> *Response: Yes, of course. Firstly, they can change and develop their self-aware-ness. Secondly, participating in meetings and trainings will help them to get useful information that they can use in practice.* (Interview with Malika Djulaeva, Tolman village, Kyrgyzstan, 4 March 2014)

Malika Djulaeva identified the development of self-awareness, or 'power-within', as the first reason why farmers should participate in trainings about the efficient use of irrigation water. She prioritised this ahead of the practical information the training was ostensibly organised to provide. In short, it could be argued that we are measuring the wrong things because we are too focused on what can be readily counted and on measuring results according to a very limited list of objectives. This brings us back to the women with whom we work. If we take the issue of their empowerment seriously, not only with regard to the activities that we implement but also in how we generate knowledge and learning about their life experiences (related to project inter-ventions), we need to reflect on our role in M&E processes as translator. Does it have an empowering, or a disempowering, effect?

Acknowledgements

We are extremely grateful to the editor, Caroline Sweetman, for all her very helpful and insightful suggestions on a first draft of this paper – resulting in major improvements to the thrust of its main argument. We would also like to thank Fenneke Reysoo, Senior Lecturer at the Department of Anthropology and Sociology of Development of the Graduate Institute, Geneva, for rapidly reading and commenting on the revised draft of the paper at very short notice. Given that the three projects discussed in the paper are all funded – in full or in part – by the SDC, we would like to acknowledge the role played by this agency in the generation of the data presented. Nevertheless, the analysis and the arguments presented are those of the authors alone.

Notes

1. Beneficiary assessment (BA) is described by the World Bank as 'system-atic consultation with project beneficiaries and other stakeholders to help them identify and design development activities, signal any potential

constraints to their participation, and obtain feedback on reactions to an intervention during implementation. BA is an investigation of the perceptions of a systematic sample of beneficiaries and other stakeholders to ensure that their concerns are heard and incorporated into project and policy formulation. The general purposes of a BA are to (1) undertake systematic listening, which 'gives voice' to poor and other hard-to-reach beneficiaries, highlighting constraints to beneficiary participation, and (2) obtain feedback on interventions. BA is a qualitative method of investigation and evaluation that relies primarily on three data collection techniques: in-depth conversational interviewing around key themes or topics; focus group discussions; and direct observation and participant observation (in which the investigator lives in the community for a short time) (http://web.worldbank.org/WBSITE/EXTERNAL/TOPICS/EXTSOCIALDEV /0,contentMDK:21233768~menuPK:3291499~page PK:64168445~piPK:64 168309~theSitePK:3177395,00.html, last checked by the authors 25 April 2014). For more information, see also Salmen (1995), and for practical examples, www.poverty-wellbeing.net/en/Home/Addressing_Poverty_in_ Practice/Beneficiary_Assessment (last checked by the authors May 2014).

2. Deep inequalities between different social groups have been a factor behind the long-standing communist movement in Nepal, which has taken different forms over the years. Between 1996 and 2006, Nepal's Maoist movement waged a 'People's War' against the then Royal Government of Nepal with the aim of overthrowing the monarchy, establishing a 'People's Republic', and realising their 40-point list of demands (a significant number of which relate to issues of inequality) (for more information, see Hutt 2004).

3. We are making a generalisation here, as the feasibility of women's involvement varies by value chain. For example, fishing is highly male dominated, requiring access to a boat and mobility during the hours of darkness, in addition to specialist skills and knowledge. For a woman to take up fishing would be extremely daring, and invite negative reaction. By contrast, the project has supported women in bullock fattening – including minority, Hindu women (although Hindus eschew beef, raising animals for this purpose is not necessarily seen negatively). Whilst women attended trainings and raised the bulls, it was found that often their husbands took over the marketing side, negotiating prices and receiving the payment. Whether this resulted in women seeing no reward for their efforts, or in gaining respect and greater negotiation power in household decision-making, depended on the particular couple dynamics. Project staff observed, nevertheless, that the likelihood of the latter outcome was greater where awareness-raising on gendered roles had been conducted.

4. UN Women defines gender-responsive budgeting as 'government planning, programming and budgeting that contributes to the advancement of gender equality and the fulfillment of women's rights. It entails identifying and reflecting needed interventions to address gender gaps in sector and local government policies, plans and budgets. GRB also aims to analyze the gender-differentiated impact of revenue-raising policies and the allocation of domestic resources and Official Development Assistance' (www.gender-budgets.org/).

5. The logical framework is a planning, management, monitoring, and evaluation tool that summarises a project's basic intervention logic in a matrix showing the causal connection between the activities and inputs to be provided from the project to its intended achievements of goals on outcome and impact level. It also provides the necessary qualitative and quantitative indicators and measurement methods and sources for assuring the completion of foreseen objectives and the important risks and assumptions (see www.zewo.ch/impact/en/ or Department for International Development, www.gov.uk/government/uploads/system/uploads/attachment_data/file/253889/using-revised-logical-framework-external.pdf, last checked by the authors May 2014).

6. A tracer study 'tracks down a group of graduated trainees who have participated in VET (Vocational Education and Training) programmes in specific trades and explores their current and past employment activities, any possible effects of the training/studies on their income, their satisfaction with the job, the quality and relevance of training received and the interrelation between their studies/training and work among other factors' (see Macchi *et al.* 2009, 3).

References

Bennett, Lynn (2006) *Unequal Citizens: Gender, Caste and Ethnic Exclusion in Nepal*, Kathmandu: DFID/World Bank.

Bhagowalia, Priya, Purnima Menon, Agnes R. Quisumbing, and Vidhya Soundararajan (2012) 'What dimensions of women's empowerment matter most for child nutrition? Evidence using nationally representative data from Bangladesh' IFPRI Discussion Paper01192, Washington, DC: IFPRI.

Dee, Jupp and Sohen Ibn Ali (2010) 'Measuring Empowerment? Ask Them: Quantifying qualitative outcomes from people's own analysis', SIDA Studies in Evaluation 2010/1, Stockholm: Swedish International Development Cooperation Agency.

Eyben, Rosalind, Irene Guijit, Chris Roche, Cathy Shutt, and Bendan Whitty (2013) 'The Politics of Evidence Conference Report', report on the conference 'The Big Push Forward' held at the Institute of Development Studies, Sussex on 23–24 April 2013, http://bigpushforward.net/archives/2405 (last checked by the authors May 2014).

Hutt, Michael (ed.) (2004) *Himalayan People's War: Nepal's Maoist Rebellion*, Bloomington, IN: Indiana University Press.

Jafa, Sayantani (2002) 'Between identities: women in post-communist Kosovo', *Indian Journal of Gender Studies* 9(1): 81–87.

Jayaratne, Toby Epstein and Abigail J. Stewart (1991) 'Quantitative and qualitative methods in the social sciences: current feminist issues and practical strategies', in Mary Margaret Fonow and Judith A. Cook (eds.) *Beyond Methodology: Feminist Scholarship as Lived Research*, Bloomington IN: Indiana University Press, 85–106.

Kabeer, Naila (1998) '"Can buy me love"? Re-evaluating the empowerment potential of loans to women in rural Bangladesh', *Discussion Paper 363*, Brighton: Institute of Development Studies.

Kabeer, Naila (1999) 'Resources, agency, achievements: reflections on the measurement of women's empowerment', *Development and Change* 30(3): 435–64.

Kabir, Md. Humayan and Zenebe B. Uraguchi (2013) 'Experiences with the DCED standard for results measurement: the case of Samriddhi in Bangladesh', paper presented at the Global Seminar on Results Measurement 24–26 March 2014, Bangkok, Dhaka: HELVETAS Swiss Intercooperation Bangladesh.

Kroesschell, Celestine (2012) *Gender in Municipal Plans and Budgets: Manual with Practical Guidelines on Gender Responsive Planning and Budgeting at Local Level*, Pristina: HELVETAS Swiss Intercooperation.

Macchi, Mirjam, Bettina Jenny, and Kurt Wilhelm (2009) *Measuring Education's Path to Prosperity: Tracer Studies for Vocational Education and Training Programmes – A Practical Tool Kit*, Zurich: Helvetas.

Mahmud, Simeen, Nirali M. Shah, and Stan Becker (2012) 'Measurement of women's empowerment in rural Bangladesh', *World Development* 40(3): 610–19.

Mays, N. and C. Pope (2000) 'Qualitative research in health care. Assessing quality in qualitative research', *British Medical Journal* 320: 50–52.

McIntyre, Lynne, Patricia Thille, and Jennifer M. Hatfield (2013) 'Interrogating progress indicators of the third Millennium Development Goal from the viewpoint of ultrapoor Bangladeshi female heads of household', *Canadian Journal of Development Studies/ Revue Canadienne d'Études du Développement* 34(4): 447–60.

Moser, Annalise (2007) *Gender and Measurements of Change: Overview report*, Sussex: BRIDGE, IDS.

Mosse, David and David Lewis (2006) *Development Brokers and Translators: The Ethnography of Aid and Agencies*, Bloomfield, CT: Kumarian Press.

Murray Li, Tania (2007) *The Will to Improve: Governmentality, Development and the Practice of Politics*, Durham, NC: Duke University Press.

Oakley, Ann (2000) *Experiments in Knowing: Gender and Method in the Social Sciences*, Cambridge: Polity.

Rowlands, Jo (1997) *Questioning Empowerment: Working with Women in Honduras*, Oxford: Oxfam.

Salmen, Lawrence F. (1995) *Beneficiary Assessment: An Approach Described*. Environment Department Paper Number 23, July 1995, Washington, DC: The World Bank.

Sharma, Jeevan R. and Antonio Donini (2010) *Towards a "Great Transformation"? The Maoist Insurgency and Local Perceptions of Social Transformation in Nepal*, Medford, MA: Feinstein International Centre, Tufts University.

Stern, Elliot, Nicoletta Stame, John Mayne, Kim Forss, Rick Davies, and Barbara Befani (2012) 'Broadening the Range of Designs and Methods for Impact Evaluations', DFID *Working Paper 38*, London: DFID.

United Nations Population Fund (UNFPA) (2005) *Gender Based Violence in Kosovo*, Pristina: UNFPA.

About the authors

Jane Carter is Gender and Social Equity Coordinator at HELVETAS Swiss Intercooperation, Switzerland. Postal address: Helvetas Swiss Intercooperation, Maulbeerstrasse 10, PO Box 6724, 3001 Bern, Switzerland. Corresponding author email: jane.carter@helvetas.org

Sarah Byrne is an Advisor for Local Governance and Civil Society at HELVETAS Swiss Intercooperation, Switzerland.

Kai Schrader is an Advisor for Learning and Evaluation at HELVETAS Swiss Intercooperation, Switzerland.

Humayun Kabir is Monitoring Specialist for Market Systems Development at HELVETAS Swiss Intercooperation Bangladesh.

Zenebe Bashaw Uraguchi is Advisor for Market Systems Development at HELEVTAS Swiss Intercooperation Bangladesh, but will shortly be taking up the position of Senior Adviser, Value Chains and Market Development, based in Switzerland.

Bhanu Pandit is Monitoring and Evaluation Officer at HELVETAS Swiss Intercooperation Nepal.

Badri Manandhar is Governance and Peace Programme Coordinator at HELVETAS Swiss Intercooperation Nepal.

Merita Barileva is a Programme Officer at HELVETAS Swiss Intercooperation, Kosovo.

Norbert Pijls is a Project Manager at HELVETAS Swiss Intercooperation, Kosovo.

Pascal Fendrich is a Governance Advisor and Deputy Coordinator for West Africa at HELVETAS Swiss Intercooperation, Switzerland.

CHAPTER 9

Using the Social Relations Approach to capture complexity in women's empowerment: using gender analysis in the Fish on Farms project in Cambodia

Emily Hillenbrand, Pardis Lakzadeh, Ly Sokhoin, Zaman Talukder, Timothy Green and Judy McLean[1]

Abstract

Gender-analysis frameworks and tools provide a pre-designed methodology which can be used for the purposes of monitoring, evaluation, and learning, as well as for research undertaken for other reasons by planners, practitioners, and academic researchers. This chapter focuses on the use of Naila Kabeer's concept, the Social Relations Approach, to frame a baseline gender analysis of a food security project undertaken in Cambodia. The Fish on Farms project was designed to establish evidence of the impact of homestead food production, which included fishponds, on nutritional status, food security, food intake, and livelihoods. Integral to the objectives was the need to understand how the project activities affect gender equality and the empowerment of women. The Social Relations Approach was chosen to explore gender relations in context, and to understand better the subjective meanings of empowerment and the pathways to it.

Keywords: gender analysis, Social Relations Approach, food security, homestead food production, gender planning

Introduction

Gender analysis is a critical element of development planning, policy, and practice. Many examples exist of projects which have foundered on lack of understanding of the gender division of labour and power relations. In response to growing awareness of the link between gender inequality and poverty, and in response to lobbying from feminists and women's movements in the global South and North, development organisations adopted gender-analysis frameworks and tools to help them undertake gender analysis as part of their project planning, implementation, and evaluation.[2]

http://dx.doi.org/10.3362/9781780447049.009

It is essential to see the selection of a gender-analysis framework as a highly political decision – not as a mere technocratic choice. Different gender-analysis frameworks and tools have strengths and weaknesses, and reflect a particular understanding of the relationships between gender roles and gender inequality, and between gender inequality and the economic and social marginalisation of households and communities. This chapter focuses on the operationalisation of Naila Kabeer's (1994) Social Relations Approach (SRA) to carry out a baseline gender analysis of a livelihoods-based food security intervention, the Fish on Farms (FoF) research project in Cambodia.

The 22-month FoF project began in June 2012.[3] FoF is an intervention focusing on improving the food security, nutritional status, and the livelihoods of food-insecure households in Cambodia, by using homestead food production (HFP).[4] FoF aims to generate rigorous scientific evidence demanded by the development community on whether a food-based, livelihoods intervention can have a measurable impact on food security and nutrition, particularly for women and young children. But in addition, designers of the project anticipate that this livelihoods-based intervention could and should have wider impact on the lives of women in particular, furthering gender equality and the empowerment of women. A crucial second objective of the baseline research was therefore to assess the impact of FoF on women's empowerment, and to gain a greater understanding of gender relations in the Cambodian context. The hypothesis of the HFP model was that the principal routes to women's empowerment are through increased human capital (knowledge of sustainable food production and caregiving practices), and through increased control over income from sales of surplus fish or vegetables, which was thought to allow women greater potential influence over household decisions (primarily around food production and consumption).

The baseline gender analysis which we are discussing in this chapter offered an opportunity to explore gender relations in context, and to understand better the subjective meanings of empowerment and the likely pathways to it. The first section of this chapter briefly focuses on why we chose Naila Kabeer 's SRA, reasoning that it offered a better way forward for monitoring, evaluation, and learning (MEL) of projects aiming to support women's empowerment than other gender-analysis tools and frameworks. We then discuss the FoF project and its different research objectives. We share the FoF gender analysis, and highlight a few of the findings that emerged from this process that might not have surfaced through other methodologies. We discuss some of the practical challenges and methodological implications of applying this approach as a gender learning tool, both for the project and for development organisations.

Gender-analysis frameworks and the SRA

The range of gender-analysis frameworks developed over the decades have different characteristics reflecting the different organisational context in which each was developed; different attitudes to the role of women in development, and the role of development in the lives of women; and difference on the question of whether and how development agencies should engineer, or stimulate, change in gender relations. Categories and terms used in the different gender-analysis frameworks reflect very different understandings of women's interests and needs, the relationship between gender inequality and poverty, and understandings of poverty itself and its causes. Often there is a focus on women only, rather than on the social and economic dynamics of gender relations; a lack of focus on the underlying beliefs which enforce gender inequality; and lack of attention to the underlying unequal power relations which explain and perpetuate gendered roles and responsibilities. Much depends on the skill and motivation of the development planner; the use of some gender-roles analyses can reflect a 'tick-box' approach that shuts down the questioning and essentially political lens which is needed when working towards gender inequality and the empowerment of women (Hochfeld and Bassadien 2007; MacDonald et al. 1999).

In addition, the fact that gender-analysis frameworks tend to focus on a 'snapshot' of gender issues can create a static understanding of gender roles and relations that may fail to capture the dynamic nature of gendered social relations (March et al. 1999). A focus on assessing gender roles and gender gaps suggests straightforward implementation solutions – through asset, skill, or social capital provision. However, failure to understand the dynamic nature of gendered relations and the subtleties and complexities of bargaining processes can lead planners to misinterpret the ways an intervention may affect men and women. These outcomes may not necessarily represent a step backwards for women; they may be an indication of positive bargaining processes in which women use the resources provided through the project to obtain a meaningful achievement (Okali 2012). However, MEL needs to be founded on more accurate information about women's interests, needs, and preferences in order to avoid women needing to subvert projects to gain outcomes that do not fit with the planners' theories of change and measures of empowerment.

In our baseline gender analysis of the FoF project, outlined in the next section, we sought to adapt and operationalise key concepts from the SRA. In contrast to many of the gender-analysis frameworks which focus on roles and responsibilities rather than power relations, Naila Kabeer 's SRA is a consciously feminist approach. It aims to capture the complexity of gender–power relations, the gendered nature of institutions, and the interactions between policies and practices at different institutional locations. However, this approach is far less frequently used by practitioners than more conventional gender-analysis frameworks, which is likely to be partly due to that fact that it is less prescriptive, tries to challenge practitioners not to lose sight of complexity, and the fact that it focuses beyond the grassroots level of household and community to other structural systems that produce and reproduce inequality, including the state and the market.

We wanted to understand how women involved in FoF defined well-being, but in addition we aimed for a richer understanding of how social differences and inequalities (in roles, responsibilities, claims, power) are produced and reproduced in the Cambodian context, and to predict better how the availability of new livelihood resources directed to women through FoF might dislocate or challenge these institutions. In the SRA, Naila Kabeer 'challeng[es] the myth of ideological neutrality, [arguing] that institutions produce, reinforce, and reproduce social difference and inequalities' (March *et al.* 1999, 105). The SRA focuses on gender biases and norms at the institutional locations of the state, market, community, and family/household. It emphasises the need to focus on change over time, and encourages reflection on the immediate, intermediate, and structural causes of inequalities at the different institutional levels.

The SRA is discussed in detail in Naila Kabeer 's now classic text Reversed Realities (Kabeer 1994). It employs five key concepts to capture the complex power dynamics between women and men, and analyses the gendered nature of social institutions. While poor people rely on networks of social relations to survive, social relationships can also reinforce inequality and unequal access to resources. The SRA encourages support to women to foster relationships of solidarity, and challenge and transform relationships which reproduce and maintain inequality. The end goal of the SRA is to help design programmes and policies that enable women to be agents of their own development (March *et al.* 1999). However, the SRA presents some methodological challenges for practitioners. The complexity and multiple levels of analysis, and the focus on gendered structures and institutions, are holistic and theoretically satisfactory but challenging to apply, particularly in a participatory manner.

The FoF project, and our gender baseline research

The FoF project uses a rigorous scientific design; it has been set up as a randomised control trial, and its primary purpose is to measure the impact of two models of HFPon reducing undernutrition among women and children. One is purely focusing on horticulture, while the other adds aquaculture (fish-farming). There is also a control group.

A total of 900 women farmers with children under five were randomly assigned to one of three equal-sized groups of 300 participants each. The first group of 300 participants is following a plant-based horticultural model, promoting home gardens and increased consumption of plant-based micronutrients. The second group is participating in an intervention promoting both home gardens and small-scale aquaculture, to increase access to and intake of animal-source foods. The third group is a control group. Within the two intervention arms, 30 demonstration farms and/or fish-ponds have been established, with one demonstration farm for every ten target beneficiaries. Technical information on aquaculture or horticulture production, nutrition, and infant and young child feeding practices (IYCF) are delivered to the target groups through on-site demonstrations, group sessions, or house-to-house counselling visits.

The baseline–endline survey instruments are designed to gather information on dietary intake and food security using standardised measures including a 24-hour food recall, food production, income, water and sanitation practices, as well as current knowledge, attitudes, and practices on nutrition, aquaculture, and home gardening. Also collected at the baseline stage were indicators of nutritional status of women and children, including biochemical markers for vitamin A and iron status, and anthropometric measures for women and children from which to assess change over time.

The project baseline gender analysis, using the SRA together with Participatory Rural Appraisal (PRA) tools,[5] was carried out within the first six months of the project. It was hoped that this would generate lessons for the project's behaviour-change communication (BCC) strategy, which aimed to support women to adopt better nutrition and caregiving practices. The idea was that the gender analysis would identify entry points for contesting unequal norms and power relations at the household, market, and community levels. We sought to understand processes of symbolic and material renegotiation of gender norms and practices over time. We looked to understand how the project's livelihood intervention fitted into the broader livelihood strategy and economic context, to focus on men's and women's roles in both productive and reproductive work, and to examine the symbolic meanings attached to these roles. We sought to define women's strategic interests, including their own definitions of empowerment and improved well-being. We wanted to examine the conflict and co-operation inherent in gender relations, and to identify the driving forces and processes for positive change. Given that Cambodian women ostensibly control household finances, a particular area of interest was to see what it meant in terms of power relations for women to be in control of income, how and whether this was linked to decision-making control, and how it fitted into and influenced women's bargaining power and strategies. Did this income control have an impact on autonomy? What impact did it have on conflict and co-operation in intra-household relations?

Outside the scope of the project, we knew also that the findings could be reflected on, and insights applied to validate or refine some of the organisation's indicators of women's empowerment used in its standard baseline and endline instruments. In addition, because implementing staff had limited experience of working on gender issues, engaging them in this inquiry was seen as an opportunity to expand their capacity to understand gender relations and thus to implement a more gender-aware project.

In the next section, we focus on the methods we used in our gender analysis in some detail, showing how the SRA and PRA tools were the foundation of the methodology.

Gender analysis methodology and design

The gender analysis was designed and led by Helen Keller International's (HKI) Regional Gender Coordinator (the first author), and was carried out by a team of 11 staff from the FoF project (including both HKI and local NGO staff). Two University of British Columbia students participated in the fieldwork and also assisted in translation, analysis, and write-up of the report.

A four-day training workshop was held in Phnom Penh. The training covered gender analysis key concepts, and allowed participants to practise semi-structured interview skills and use of PRA tools. The fieldwork was carried out in two FonF districts in Prey Veng province,[6] a highly food-insecure area with high rates of malnutrition.[7]

Three adjacent clusters, each consisting of ten women farmers from a given village model farm site, were selected at random and invited to participate in the research by staff from FoF. Participants came from each of the two operational arms of the project: horticulture-only and horticulture plus aquaculture. At each research site, approximately 60 respondents took part in the research. Some of them participated in multiple interviews and exercises. Participatory discussions were held separately with groups of women involved in the project as beneficiaries, their husbands, and in some cases, grandmothers. All interviews were recorded, and respondents gave informed consent prior to the discussions.

Research tools and questions

The interview questions were structured around the use of PRA tools to encourage dialogue and involvement of the respondents in the research process. The research focused primarily on the family/household, while also looking at how gender norms and rules play out at the institutional level of the market and in selected community institutions (Table 9.1).

Analysing and applying the findings

The interviews were recorded and later transcribed from Khmer to English, and coded for cross-referencing. However, primary analysis of the data was conducted in the field with the research team. Each day of data collection was followed by a day of analysis, which involved team members consolidating and checking their notes and following structured analytical guidelines to summarise the critical content and trends, triangulating the perspectives of the different age and gender groups. Following the analysis in the field and the preliminary write-up, a core team of HKI and Organisation to Develop Our Village (ODOV) staff (who are responsible for implementation) participated in a group workshop to reflect on the consolidated gender issues that surfaced during the research. Together, they prioritised the norms and ways of behaving that they considered critical to address through the FoF communications strategy.

The analysis did not perfectly apply all levels of the Social Analysis framework. However, we primarily applied the Social Relations analysis (concept 2 in the SRA, see March *et al.* 1999) and Institutional analysis (concept 3, *ibid.*), examining the institution of the household/family through the interrelated dimensions of social relationships (rules, activities, resources, people, activities, and power). We also focused on the dynamic characteristics of gender

Table 9.1 Tools and topics.

Historical timeline of gender trends. Administered to male and female elders, female beneficiaries, and male spouses, the historical timeline asked respondents to recall a chronological history of significant trends in gender relations and norms in their communities in their lifetimes.

Social relations aspects:
Typically used in sustainable livelihoods assessments to look at environmental and natural resource management trends in a community, this timeline captured the processes by which gender norms change. It highlighted the role of institutions (state, NGOs) in promoting change; the power holders in the community who resist and/or promote change; and the consequences for gender 'rebels' or those who challenge gender norms.

Seasonal calendar. Men and women created an agriculture calendar to describe agriculture practices, income-generating activities, food insecurity, peak labour periods, and challenges in agriculture.

Social relations aspects:
While the project focuses on a single, women-focused livelihood activity (aquaculture, homestead food production), this tool situated that activity within its broader livelihoods context and looked at interactions and interrelations between the livelihood activities in which men and women engage. The questions probed how women and men valued and balanced income and consumption needs; how women and men got technical support for their activities; the labour intensity of different activities; and the importance of non-economic uses (gift-giving). By asking men as well as women about their priorities and challenges, the research sought to identify areas of co-operation and agreement, as well as specific areas where women wanted to negotiate change.

Fish-ranking exercise. Using pictures of the fish species being promoted by the FoF project, the respondents (beneficiaries only) ranked the different species according to a number of factors, including taste, ease of rearing, marketability, and nutritional value.

Social relations aspects:
While the primary purpose of this exercise was to identify potential barriers to the acceptability of the fish species provided by the project, the questioning also explored women's subjective notions of health and well-being, and surfaced their simultaneous interests in pursuing aquaculture as a market venture as well as subsistence and consumption activity. It explored intra-household food distribution and the gendered food taboos that might influence consumption or sale of different species.

Venn diagram on market access. Men and women constructed a Venn diagram illustrating the institutions that they considered most important for marketing produce and purchasing inputs. The discussions covered their relative access to these institutions and illustrated differences between men's and women's marketing strategies and challenges.

Social relations aspects:
Recognising institutions as gendered, the tools look specifically at how gender rules are at play in the relationships that men and women are able to form to get access to different livelihood and financial services.

Pocket chart on household responsibilities. Respondents listed all of the productive and reproductive tasks carried out within the household and allocated each task to the 'pocket' of the person typically responsible for these tasks. The chart illustrated the gendered division of labour and disparities in workload distribution.

(Continue)

Table 9.1 (*Continued*)

Social relations aspects:
While this tool is used in gender trainings to highlight disparities in workloads and can emphasise an overly oppositional understanding of the relationship between men and women, the questioning also looked at situations in which gender responsibilities can and are being challenged or renegotiated. In particular, it explored the entry points for furthering positive engagement of men in caregiving.

Asset management diagram. Men and women illustrated all of the productive assets owned by the household and drew lines depicting which household members had management responsibilities, control, and decision-making authority over the assets.

Social relations aspects:
Rather than focusing on who owns what, the inquiry focused on the meanings women assigned to equitable decision-making control, and it probed the hidden strategies by which they bargained over the use and control of assets. How are 'joint decisions' defined? What are the meanings of a satisfactory decision-making process for women? Do women really value *autonomous* control over assets? It highlighted the unequal power relationships in bargaining processes, but also the cultural norms and hidden negotiations that women draw on to place limitations on men's unilateral decision-making.

Body maps of gender norms. Women and men illustrated a picture of the 'ideal woman' and 'ideal man', respectively. Through explanations of the drawings, they explored the customary and contemporary expectations for men and women and the ways in which they adhere to and renegotiate the traditional cultural codes.

Social relations aspects:
Often used in reproductive health analysis, the body maps sought to identify hegemonic gender norms and values, as well as the variations and spectrum of these norms. The inquiry probed the contemporary significance of the traditional behaviour codes for men and women (*chbab srey/chbab ppro*[a]); how these are reproduced by family and state institutions; and how individuals and groups renegotiate and reinterpret the codes to their own benefit and their own identity.

Focus group discussions (FGDs) and key informant interviews. During the research process, three interviews were added to further probe some of the issues that arose in the discussions. These included FGDs with beneficiary women on *financial management*; an FGD with grandmothers on *childcare and perceptions of nutrition*; and an FGD and key informant interview with beneficiaries and community leaders on the issue of domestic violence.

Social relations aspects:
Women in Cambodia ostensibly and traditionally have control over household money-management, but in this analysis, we looked at what that means in terms of relative influence and status within the household. Rather than focusing on whose money buys what, the financial management interviews explored the grey areas behind women's traditional responsibility for controlling household finances. It looked at the limitations of that authority, when and where that responsibility may be overridden by the male head of household, and how they negotiate for outcomes. It explored how threats of gender-based violence related to decision-making control, but it also illustrated how men themselves sometimes rely on gender narratives to set spending limits with their peers in support of the household well-being.

[a]Cambodia has a traditional moral code of conduct for women, the chbab srey, and a similar code for men, the chbab pro, which were written into verse in the late 19th century and are still promoted in the public schools. The codes prescribe a subordinate, shy, and subservient role for women, and a strong decision-making role for men. Women are told to remain silent and never challenge their husbands, no matter how he acts, which reinforces the high tolerance for violence against women.

relations of institutions – specifically their ability to adapt to changes in the external context through a process of bargaining and negotiation (*ibid.*). We looked at how changes in other institutions such as community and international NGOs, the state, and its education and gender policies as well as the market intersected with the institutional rules at the household and family level. It is not within the scope of this paper to discuss the findings in detail. While our analysis does not capture the level of detail and complexity and broader institutional scope of the framework, it brought out key relational aspects that that might otherwise have been missed in a roles analysis.

Focusing on relationships between people and their relationship to resources and activities

The analysis focused on relationships and negotiations at the family/household level, and their engagement in the livelihood strategy (which encompasses caregiving). It revealed how institutionalised gender rules, in particular the *chbab srey* and *chbab ppro* shape the type of activities in which women engage and the resources and decisions that they control. The traditional codes of conduct for men and women, still transmitted through the state education system and through intergenerational cultural transfer, shape and reinforce power inequalities within the household and community, often limiting women's well-being, autonomy, and livelihood choices.

In general, the codes were seen as relevant and appropriate, particularly the division of labour and the expectation for the man to be the breadwinner. However, men's and women's understandings of these codes also revealed how these meanings are being renegotiated by women and men to accommodate modern identities and livelihood opportunities. Understanding these values and the process helped us identify entry points to challenge harmful norms through the BCC strategy. For example, the majority of respondents (both men and women) welcomed the 'sexy clothes' and modern styles, feeling that the traditional dress code and the imperative for women to walk slowly and speak softly were impractical and out of keeping with modern, working life. For women, codes related to modest dress, soft voice, and not visiting with the neighbours no longer seemed practical or modern in the context of women's income-earning role. As one woman noted:

> Women can go far away from home now to make an income. The way of speaking has also changed. We don't speak as softly anymore ... We also need to know how to talk back with reason to other people. And we also walk faster now, because we need to catch up with other people. If they walk this way, we have to walk this way also.

Thanks to their income-earning role, women felt at liberty to disregard some of the gender rules about their mobility, patience, and unconditional reverence for the husbands. Before, as one group discussion explained, an ideal woman was expected to sit at home and never visit the neighbours, for fear of 'bringing the fire outside' (taking family problems outside). She was expected to be patient and always to accept the husband's behaviour, no matter what. Nowadays, though, women see the need to discuss business matters with other women and feel more comfortable asserting themselves when they believe they are in the right. One woman summarised it as follows:

> When we are home, we get bored, we also need to [visit the neighbours to] discuss ways to make money. Being patient is also hard to do because if the husband keeps on creating conflict, like when he is drunk and angry ... then we need to fight back.

Women reported that they were also grateful for the social freedom to talk about previously taboo health topics, particularly around reproductive health.

Revealing how these relationships are reworked through institutions such as the state or the market

The analysis looked at how gender rules are produced and reinforced in the community and marketplace, shaping men's and women's production, livelihood, and caregiving choices and aspirations. It showed how the gendered institution of the market is offering new livelihood opportunities. In particular, trans-national migration for men and garment work opportunities for women. These gendered migration flows are shaped by traditional gender norms but also contain the seeds for renegotiating intra-household power relations. Gendered migration patterns offered physically risky transnational work opportunities (in Thailand) for men in the fishing sector, while the garment industry, in contrast, primarily recruited dexterous (and docile) young women. The women reported that they often reserved a part of their income for themselves, and could demand greater household support from spouses. In addition, these multi-local livelihood strategies were rapidly transforming nutrition and caregiving practices, as more and more children were left in the care of grandparents.

Showing change over time

Adding the historical dimension of the analysis illustrated the shifting power relationships between older and younger generations, and pulled out competing contemporary narratives of an 'ideal man', each of which has a different implication for women's well-being and autonomy. This perspective helped illustrate where the project could build on momentum towards equitable gender relations.

For example, alongside evidence of strictly hierarchical gender relationships, gender-based violence, and expectations that women should stay home as long as men have work, there was also a recurrent theme that 'women and men have equal rights', an idea that seems to have been promoted through NGOs, state policies, and by community-level authorities, some of who had received training on gender and on intervening in cases of domestic violence. Many associated this idea of women's rights with Cambodia's rapid economic development, and saw greater gender equality as a marker of modernity. One respondent challenged traditional views of women, explicitly equating this belief with lack of education:

> *Before, they said that having a daughter is like a having a pot of fish paste at home, but having a son is like having a piece of gold. If it is dropped in mud, it is still gold and has the same quality. But for the woman, she can drop from a ten karat gold to eight karat if she made a mistake. In the past, they always placed the man higher than women because they didn't know any better.*

Through interactions at the macro-economic level, government initiatives, and NGO interventions, the cultural environment currently appears conducive to messages promoting gender equality, and even elders appeared to be receptive to such ideas.

Highlighting the nuances and complexities of gender relations

Looking beyond who typically 'does what' in the household, the analysis refined how women in the target groups define equitable and harmonious relationships. In addition to examining the power inequalities between men and women, the analysis showed how gendered beliefs and norms about masculinity and appropriate roles for men are reinforced and negotiated through social relationships between men.

For men, there was a notable struggle over the traditional social prohibitions on alcohol and gambling, which they knew to be inscribed in the *chhbap prro*. The men referred back to the *chhbap prro* and considered these prohibitions against alcohol to be appropriate rules for society:

> *Alcohol can make a person lose his consideration, leading to violence, wasting money, fighting with others and being unhealthy.*

At the same time, drinking with male friends had become a common way to celebrate any event – a wedding, getting a job. Men explained that if they walked by a peer or neighbour drinking, they would be socially obligated to join in, and to take turns buying rounds among the peers. One man stated:

> *In the past, a man who drinks alcohol would not be accepted as a son-in-law by any family ... Now it is the way to show regard to others.*

Many sought alternatives to this pressure, which challenged their financial responsibilities as heads of household. Some used their wives' traditional responsibility as money managers as a legitimate excuse to limit the amount of money that they could spend in a sitting. However, women noted that they had limited effective control; if men asked for money, women were obliged to give it.

This shared concern between men and women, though challenging to address, offers entry points for a communications strategy that draws on the appeal of a positive traditional masculinity that is in line with women's aspirations for more co-operative and respectful intra-household relations.

Listening to women's own aspirations and definitions of empowerment

One of the most frequently overlooked dimensions of development programmes is the need to define indices of change which are appropriate for the context. This involves listening closely – and responding to – what women (and men) themselves consider to be empowering and positive indicators of change. The core concept of the SRA as conceptualised by Naila Kabeer is development as well-being (autonomy, human security, and dignity, and not simply economic development). The gender analysis identified priorities of women that were entirely absent from the project's measures of change or implementation strategy. For example, women identified a need for a reduction in gender-based violence and men's alcohol use. The respondents also offered workable and practical solutions to the problems, through existing state and NGO institutions. The analysis also identified that men as well as women saw this as a challenge of development and welcomed solutions.

Outcomes of the gender analysis

Following the gender analysis process, the core HKI and ODOV team spent a two-day workshop prioritising the key findings and identifying how they could be addressed and integrated within the nutrition and gender BCC strategy. The strategy, drawing from the gender analysis findings, identified the priority issues (as defined by the respondents and in line with the project goals), to be: unequal decision-making influence, unequal workload sharing, unequal responsibilities and knowledge around caregiving, and prevalence of alcohol misuse and gender-based violence. The strategy then identified the intermediate and underlying norms or beliefs (from the research) that were used to justify and uphold these inequalities and that the project could try to challenge (for instance, 'women's work is considered light, and women do not respect men's caregiving capacity', or 'women are expected to be docile. It is women's responsibility to create harmony, even in situations of violence').

Next, we outlined women's definitions of well-being and their aspirations for the project. We transformed these into a set of gender goals, to transform the priority challenges and promote more equitable practices. Finally, we identified a series of specific gender actions that could be integrated into the nutrition and BCC activities (these included a joint budgeting exercise, including grandmothers in cooking demonstrations, encouraging men's caregiving support, linking to gender-based violence organisations, developing a nutrition game that also included costs of healthy foods, snack foods, and alcohol). Using data from the field research, we also crafted tentative 'messages' derived from the communities that could be tested and used to transform the harmful or limiting norms and promote some of the equitable alternatives that already exist in the communities.

Conclusion: limitations and implications for future work

Conducting this process at an early stage in the project implementation, and with the participation of implementing staff, provided an opportunity to orient the project in a gender-transformative direction. The direct output of the analysis was a gender-informed BCC strategy for the project. Participation in the gender analysis was considered to be a valuable experience for the investigators involved in the process and was seen by the project implementers as an important complement to the baseline survey. As an HKI participant explained in a personal communication with the first author in December 2013:

> The critical point of the process is that all strategies to solve problems from research findings are developed by enumerators, which is feasible and adoptable by community members at research area. We learnt many useful tools such as pocket chart, venn diagram, seasonal calendar and body map. Those tools have been used with target beneficiaries. For instance, during the monthly meeting with both wife and husband of all target households in the village, we introduced them with the pocket chat of household chore, then husbands realized that their wife have done much more works than themselves. Based on the mapping conducted in every two weeks, we can see that the household works of women are being shared by other family members, especially husbands.

She added that some of the drawback to the process and methodology were that it was time-consuming and took enumerators – who are project staff – away from other start-up activities. Another challenge that was noted was that the field staff need to have good skills in facilitating and probing if respondents are to participate actively in the discussions.

Using the SRA in this way presented practical, methodological, and political choices for the organisation. First, in contrast to roles analysis, this approach requires extensive and skilful probing to capture the meanings and subtleties of bargaining strategies. It also entails a solid understanding of gender to analyse interrelations and processes of change. Working with field staff as researchers in this exercise had important payoffs in terms of expanding their own understandings of gender relations and the processes of (dis) empowerment, but particularly for staff of the same cultural upbringing as the respondents and with limited gender training background, it may have been challenging to take note of intra-household transactions that seem obvious or normal. Some richness of detail has been lost in translation and in observation. Moreover, because the research was carried out and analysed by field staff and not researchers, the quality of the data are less rigorous and hence less acceptable in the research community.

An analysis approach such as this that emphasises *processes* of gender change and the dynamic nature of gender relations and institutional changes also requires effective process-monitoring and learning tools that facilitate introspection and interpretation of changes over time. In the short duration of this project, it is not clear what changes can be expected in terms of social norms. From an organisational perspective, applying social relations concepts would entail a cultural shift from monitoring surveys focused more on adoption of production practices to a more process-oriented set of learning tools for monitoring gender change. This would also entail ongoing investment in capacity building of analytical and observation skills.

Our experience suggests the need to fine-tune some of the outcome indicators or response choices around joint decision-making that are commonly used in the survey, as well as the particular decisions included in the module. Measuring the actual meanings of decision-making, and the degree of individuals' autonomy *within* co-operative decisions, is notoriously challenging. While this analysis alone is not sufficient to reword those instruments, it does suggest a need for further analysis to fine-tune and revalidate these variables in context, so that they accurately capture progress towards women's empowerment on their own cultural terms.

We aimed to disaggregate views by generational group (interviewing grandmothers, mothers, and husbands separately). However, given that the mothers selected to participate were of similar wealth-status and age cohort, the gender analysis did not capture the intersections of class or other factors. Staff invited mothers to participate voluntarily, but self-selection may have favoured those individuals with more time, education, curiosity, or interest in gaining from the intervention. Male respondents, spouses of participants, or others who were available in the village at the time may not be representative of those who were absent and engaged in outside work. Because the researchers were new to the process, it was clear that in some sessions they failed to separate men from women or to isolate influential power holders, which resulted in a few dominant voices speaking for an entire group. Finally, although it used participatory tools and processes, the participation could best be classified as consultative, rather than co-operative. Although the results were shared back with the groups, the power to incorporate the findings and address the priorities rests unilaterally with the HKI and NGO staff implementing the project and designing the strategy – a point which has been made in the wider literature on participation in development project planning and MEL (Johnson *et al.* 2004).

Ultimately, a framework's usefulness is only as good as the analysis of the findings and the commitment to the processes of change it highlights. The challenge of any gender analysis poses an inherent dilemma, in that priorities identified may not align with the measures of success by which the project is evaluated and for which it is funded. For example, in the FoF analysis, gender-based violence (a marker of systemic gender injustice) and gendered alcohol use emerged as the participants' priorities and as indicators of empowerment. While these issues were incorporated into the FoF communications strategy, there was limited capacity to modify designs and integrate women's concerns into the programming. Addressing them effectively in future project designs could yet be perceived as mission drift (not directly enough linked to food security) or as beyond the capacity of the organisation to address.

Yet the SRA challenges the notion of gender-neutrality in all institutions, including that of the gendered implementing organisations, and by raising some gender-justice issues to be considered in future designs, using it presents opportunities for organisational reflection on the approach and the positioning of the organisation in the development space. For this reason, the SRA seems to us to present the most comprehensive framework available to us to use, and one that is most closely aligned with a notion of transformation of gendered institutions and redistribution of power.

Notes

1. Emily Hillenbrand led the FoF baseline gender analysis together with Ly Sokhoin, Deputy Program Manager at HKI, and Pardis Lakzadeh and Hellene Sarin from UBC. The FoF research is led by Judy McLean PhD, Assistant Professor UBC, Timothy Green PhD, Associate Professor, UBC; implementation is led by Zaman Talukder and Hou Kroeun of HKI.
2. For an account of this process and an introduction to some of the best known and earliest frameworks, see March *et al.* (1999).
3. FoF is led by Helen Keller International in partnership with researchers from the University of British Columbia, with WorldFish Center, Organisation to Develop Our Village, and the Cambodian Fisheries Administration of the Ministry of Agriculture, Forests, and Fisheries. The project is supported by IDRC and the Canadian Department of Foreign Affairs Trade and Development, through the Canadian International Food Security Research Fund.
4. Homestead food production (HFP) is a food-based intervention designed to promote nutrition and food security through increased availability and affordability of nutritious foods. Helen Keller International's HFP model supports home-based food production through a package of technical agriculture and small livestock support and nutrition and gender education. HKI's models in Asia have been shown to increase dietary diversity, increase women's income and control over income, and in some cases reduce anaemia.
5. Participatory Rural Appraisal (PRA) is a process of engagement with rural people to investigate, analyse, and evaluate constraints and opportunities from their perspective, and using indigenous knowledge. In livelihoods programming, commonly used PRA tools include the seasonal calendar, transect walk, Venn diagram, farm resource maps, wealth-ranking, mobility map, historical timeline of livelihood trends, preference ranking. These participatory tools validate indigenous knowledge and enable low literacy participants to analyse development challenges and opportunities.
6. Prey Veng Province in central Cambodia is categorised as chronically high food-insecure (WFP 2007). An area with currently low practices of

pond-based fish-culture, it models the consequences of the impending damming of the Mekong and its potential devastation of the Tonle Sap and those who depend on it for capture fishing.

7. Food security is defined as having adequate access to, availability, and utilisation of food at all times. Most provinces in Cambodia are considered chronically food-insecure, and malnutrition rates are severe. Nearly 10 per cent of children die before their fifth birthday, with over 30 per cent of these deaths attributed to undernutrition. Food insecurity and malnutrition in Cambodia stem, in part, from low productivity and a lack of crop diversification beyond rice. As such, poor households subsist on a diet consisting mainly of rice, which provides an estimated 70 per cent of food energy, but is low in fat, essential amino acids, and micronutrients. Animal source foods, which provide high-quality protein, essential fatty acids, and bioavailable iron and vitamin A, make up less than 9 per cent of total energy intake. Lack of dietary diversity indicates micronutrient malnutrition, contributing to anaemia and weak immune systems, and limiting child growth and cognitive development. Low fat consumption limits absorption of fat-soluble vitamins, exacerbating the problem of micronutrient malnutrition.

References

Hochfeld, Tessa and Shanana Bassadien (2007) 'Gender and Development', *Gender Research Methodologies* 15(2): 217–230.

Johnson, Nancy, Nina Lilja, Jackie Ashby and James Garcia (2004) 'The Practice of Participatory research and gender analysis in natural resource management', *Natural Resources Forum* 28(3): 198–200.

Kabeer, Naila (1994) *Reversed Realities: Gender Hierarchies in Development Thought*, London: Verso.

MacDonald, Mandy, Ellen Sprenger, and Ireen Dubel (1999) *Gender and Organizational Change: Bridging the Gap between Policy and Practice*, Amsterdam: Royal Tropical Institute.

March, Candida, Ines Smith and Maitrayee Mukhopadhya (1999) *A Guide to Gender Analysis Frameworks*, London: Oxfam GB.

Okali, Christine (2012) *Gender Analysis: Engaging with Rural Development and Agriculture Policy Processes*, FAC Working Paper 26, Brighton: Future Agricultures Constortium.

World Food Programme (2007) *Integrated Food Security and Humanitarian Phase Classification (IPC) Pilot in Cambodia*. Final Report, http://documents.wfp.org/stellent/groups/public/documents/ena/wfp128541.pdf (last checked by the authors May 2014).

About the authors

Emily Hillenbrand is currently Gender and Livelihoods Advisor for CARE USA. She designed and led the Fish on Farms gender analysis, in her previous capacity as Regional Gender Coordinator for Helen Keller

International Asia-Pacific. Postal address: 151 Ellis Street, Atlanta, GA 30303, USA. Corresponding author email: ehillenbrand@care.org

Pardis Lakzadeh is Master of Science student in the School of Public Health at the University of British Columbia, Canada.

Zaman Talukder is the Country Director in Cambodia and Regional Food Security Advisor, Asia-Pacific, for Helen Keller International. He is a Principal Investigator on the Fish on Farms Project.

Timothy Green PhD is an Associate Professor of Human Nutrition in the Faculty of Land and Food Systems at the University of British Columbia, Canada. He is a Principal Investigator on the Fish on Farms Project.

Judy McLean is Assistant Professor of Human Nutrition at the Faculty of Land and Food Systems at the University of British Columbia, Canada. She is a Co-Principal Investigator on the Fish on Farms Project.

CHAPTER 10
Resources

Compiled by Liz Cooke

Monitoring, evaluation and learning

Capturing Change in Women's Realities: A Critical Overview of Current Monitoring & Evaluation Frameworks and Approaches (2010), Srilatha Batliwala and Alexandra Pittman, Toronto: Association for Women's Rights in Development, www. awid.org/About-AWID/AWID-News/Capturing-Change-in-Women-s-Realities (last accessed April 2014), 43 pp.

In this useful paper, published by the Association for Women's Rights in Development, the authors critically engage with some of the common challenges and 'politics' associated with monitoring and evaluation (M&E) – for example, the difficulty in assessing how change happens and how gender relations have been altered; and the perception that measurement is used more as a tool of enforcement and accountability to the donor than as a means of understanding and learning what works. They identify feminist practices for engaging in M&E in order to strengthen learning and more readily capture the complex changes sought by projects aiming to support women's empowerment and gender equality. Part II of the paper offers an analysis of a large number of M&E frameworks and tools, along with some of their strengths and weaknesses in assessing women's rights and gender equality processes and impacts.

Strengthening Monitoring and Evaluation for Women's Rights: Twelve Insights for Donors (2011), Srilatha Batliwala, Toronto: Association for Women's Rights in Development, www.awid.org/Library/Strengthening-Monitoring-and-Evaluation-for-Women-s-Rights-Twelve-Insights-for-Donors (last accessed April 2014), 11 pp.

Strengthening Monitoring and Evaluation for Women's Rights: Thirteen Insights for Women's Organizations (2011), Srilatha Batliwala, Toronto: Association for Women's Rights in Development, www.awid.org/Library/Strengthening-Monitoring-and-Evaluation-for-Women-s-Rights-Thirteen-Insights-for-Women-s-Organizations (last accessed April 2014), 16 pp.

A result of the Association for Women's Rights in Development's action research undertaken during 2009 and 2010 to study the challenges faced by women's organisations and their donors in effectively monitoring and evaluating women's rights work, these two documents present short discussions

http://dx.doi.org/10.3362/9781780447049.010

around each 'insight'. The discussions serve as both valuable analyses of the challenges presented around women's rights work and monitoring and evaluation (M&E), and as a set of recommendations for working on M&E in the future. Insight number one from the paper addressing women's organisations is 'Make M&E a key ingredient in our learning and accountability', and Insight number one for donors is 'Make M&E a learning partnership, not a performance test!'

Feminist Evaluation and Research: Theory and Practice (2014) Sharon Brisolara, Denise Seigart, and Saumitra SenGupta, New York and London: The Guildford Press. ISBN: 978-1462515202.

This excellent edited collection – which is rigorous and comprehensive but accessibly and engagingly written – is divided into three sections. The first, Feminist theory, research and evaluation, provides an overview and introduction to the topic, with the following sections, Feminist evaluation in practice, and Feminist research in practice giving practical examples.

Gender and Monitoring: A Review of Practical Experiences. Paper Prepared for the Swiss Agency for Development and Co-operation (2001), Paola Brambilla, Brighton: BRIDGE, Institute of Development Studies, www.bridge.ids.ac.uk/go/home&id=52836&type=Document&langID=1 (last accessed April 2014), 25 pp.

Aiming to be a practical tool that can be used to integrate a gender approach into existing monitoring and evaluation (M&E) mechanisms, this paper first defines M&E, goes on to look at how indicators can be made gender-sensitive, who should be involved in this process, and when they should be used during the project cycle. The paper includes case studies of implementation of gender monitoring at different levels and the following recommendations are made: indicators must be both qualitative and quantitative and take account of contextual factors; there is a need for participation of women and men in the target group in M&E processes; and gender-disaggregated indicators are necessary, but not sufficient. They must be complemented by qualitative analysis and baseline data in order to track changes of gender relations.

Measuring Women's Empowerment and Social Transformation in the Post-2015 Agenda (2014), Caroline Harper, Keiko Nowacka, Hanna Alder, and Gaëlle Ferrant, London: Overseas Development Institute, www.odi.org.uk/sites/odi.org.uk/files/odi-assets/publications-opinion-files/8838.pdf (last accessed April 2014), 8 pp.

Arguing that gender equality should be central to the post-2015 development framework, and that progress on data collection in recent years has made the capture of social norms increasingly accessible, affordable, and regular, the authors of this report outline a set of transformative indicators under six key measurement areas that, taken together, can track the changes in social norms that indicate the increasing empowerment of women and girls. The authors propose a set of indicators in six measurement areas. These are: women and girls exercise choice over their sexual and reproductive integrity; women and girls enjoy freedom from violence; women and girls enjoy enhanced decision-making ability over land and assets; women attain enhanced participation in political and civic life; equal value is given to girls and boys; and unpaid care is equally distributed between women and men, and girls and boys.

The Conditions and Consequences of Choice: Reflections on the Measurement of Women's Empowerment, UNRISD Discussion Paper No. 108 (1999), Naila Kabeer, Geneva: United Nations Research Institute for Social Development, www.unrisd.org/80256B3C005BCCF9/(httpAuxPages)/31EEF181BEC398A380 256B67005B720A/$file/dp108.pdf (last accessed April 2014), 58 pp.

This paper is a very thoughtful and thorough consideration of the challenges involved in constructing indicators of women's empowerment, focusing in particular on the meanings given to these measures, and the values embedded within them – both the values of those whose lives are being assessed, and the values of those who are doing the measuring. It starts out by suggesting a three-dimensional conceptual framework for thinking about women's empowerment: 'resources' as part of the preconditions of empowerment; 'agency' as an aspect of process; and 'achievements' as a measure of outcomes. It goes on to consider the ways in which these different dimensions have been measured by economists, demographers, sociologists, and feminists. A number of key methodological points are made, in particular, the need for the cross-checking of measures, to ensure that indicators really do mean what they are intended to mean.

Measuring Empowerment: Cross-disciplinary Perspectives (2005), Deepa Narayan, Washington, DC: World Bank, https://openknowledge.worldbank.org/ bitstream/handle/10986/7441/344100PAPER0Me101Official0use0only1. pdf?sequence=1 (last accessed April 2014)

This thorough and thoughtful work considers empowerment in a range of contexts. Section Two, focusing on Gender and Household, consists of three essays: Women's Empowerment as a Variable in International Development; Measuring Women's Empowerment – Learning from Cross-national Research; and Gender, Power, and Empowerment: An Analysis of Household and Family Dynamics. Overall, the section stresses three main points. Firstly, the household is not neutral, but instead a site of unequal formal and informal rules and social norms that result in unequal power relations between women and men. Secondly, the socio-cultural context matters, and can be more important than individual traits in determining women's empowerment, and thirdly, psychological or mental space plays a key role at individual, and community level. These points help explain the author's common emphasis on women's empowerment through collective action.

Review of Evaluation Approaches and Methods Used by Interventions on Women and Girls' Empowerment (2014), Georgia Taylor and Paola Pereznieto, London: Overseas Development Institute, www.odi.org.uk/sites/odi.org.uk/files/ odi-assets/publications-opinion-files/8843.pdf (last accessed April 2014), 50 pp.

This clearly set-out review assesses the quality and effectiveness of evaluation methods and approaches used to analyse the effects of programmes to promote women and girls' economic empowerment. The review analysed evaluations that assessed some measure of women and girls' economic empowerment in one or more of the following eight thematic areas: Financial services; Business development services; Skills training; Asset provision (both financial and physical); Social protection; Unions and fair employment; Trade and access to markets; Regulatory and legal frameworks. Key findings included: mixed-methods (quantative and qualitative) evaluations were more effective in capturing changes in norms, attitudes, and behaviours associated with women's and girls' economic empowerment; data and analysis in evaluations are not generally disaggregated by age or life-cycle stages; and, in order to guide the evaluation, it is necessary to undertake a rigorous context and gender analysis and to have a Theory of Change.

Understanding and Measuring Women's Economic Empowerment: Definition, Framework and Indicators (2011), Anne Marie Golla, Anju Malhotra, Priya Nanda, and Rekha Mehra, Washington, DC: International Center for Research on Women, www.icrw.org/publications/understanding-and-measuring-womens-economic-empowerment (last accessed April 2014), 12 pp.

This very useful short report lays out fundamental concepts, including a definition of women's economic empowerment; a measurement framework that can guide the design, implementation, and evaluation of programmes aiming to empower women economically; and a set of indicators that can serve as concrete examples for developing meaningful metrics for success.

Gender Issues in Monitoring and Evaluation. Module 16 in the Gender in Agriculture Sourcebook (2009), Washington, DC: World Bank, http://siteresources.world-bank.org/INTGENAGRLIVSOUBOOK/Resources/Module16.pdf (last accessed April 2014), 142 pp.

This Module from the Gender in Agriculture Sourcebook is a particularly well-thought-out and well-designed guide to gender and monitoring, evaluation, and learning, and while concentrating on agriculture, much of the information it contains can be applied across all development sectors. The module aims to address gender concerns in designing agricultural and rural development projects and to provide ideas – indicators, principles, approaches, and practical options – for improving monitoring and evaluation of outcomes and impacts.

Gender Issues in Monitoring and Evaluation in Rural Development: A Tool Kit (2005), Washington, DC: World Bank, http://siteresources.worldbank.org/INTGENDER/ResourcesRuralM_EToolkit2005.pdf (last accessed April 2014), 24 pp.

Aimed at World Bank staff and others involved in World Bank projects, this document is a 'how to guide', walking the user through the process of creating gender-sensitive monitoring and evaluation and the integration of a participatory approach. It then provides examples from a number of rural sub-sectors (e.g. sustainable agriculture and natural resource management; and agro-enterprise development) of relevant checklists for gender-related issues and activities during the project cycle, and a framework for results and results monitoring.

'Measuring gender equality in education' (2005), Elaine Unterhalter, Chloe Challender, and Rajee Rajagopalan, in Sheila Aikman and Elaine Unterhalter (eds.) *Beyond Access: Transforming Policy and Practice for Gender Equality in Education*, Oxford: Oxfam GB, pp. 60–79. The book is available to download at no cost at http://policy-practice.oxfam.org.uk/publications/beyond-access-transforming-policy-and-practice-for-gender-equality-in-education-115410 (last accessed April 2014)

While the statistics presented here are inevitably somewhat out of date, having been published in 2005, this chapter nevertheless provides a valuable discussion of measuring gender equality in education, first critically reviewing measures of gender equality in education used by international agencies and governments, then outlining the development of an alternative measure, the Gender Equality in Education Index (GEII). The GEII aimed to include not only the number of girls attending and remaining in primary school, but also whether these girls were able to build on this, in terms of future secondary schooling, leading healthy lives, and making a reasonable living.

A Guide to Gender-analysis Frameworks (1999), Candida March, Ines Smyth, and Maitrayee Mukhopadhyay, Oxford: Oxfam GB, http://policy-practice. oxfam.org.uk/publications/a-guide-to-gender-analysis-frameworks-115397 (last accessed April 2014), 144 pp.

A variety of frameworks to analyse gender relations are used in development work. They can be helpful tools in planning gender-sensitive research projects, or in designing development interventions which address gender inequalities. Drawing on the experience of trainers and practitioners, this book contains step-by-step instructions for using different gender-analysis frameworks, and summaries of their advantages and disadvantages in particular situations. An introductory section explains the importance of gender analysis, and the role of the frameworks in development initiatives and research.

Experiments in Knowing: Gender and Method in the Social Sciences (2000), Ann Oakley, Cambridge and Malden, MA: Polity, ISBN: 97807456 22576, website: www.polity.co.uk

Exploring the history, ideology, and implications of methodology in the social and natural sciences, the author of this influential book argues that these disciplines have been subject to a process of 'gendering', which has produced an ideological reaction against, rather than a relevant understanding of, the role of 'quantitative' and experimental methods. For her, the rejection of 'quantitative' ways of knowing, in particular, prevents an understanding of both the parameters of social inequality and the effects of interventions in people's lives. As a methodological position adopted by feminists, postmodernists, and others, it obstructs the development of a critical and emancipatory social science.

Indicators for use in monitoring, evaluation, and learning

Oxfam Quick Guide to Gender-sensitive Indicators, http://policy-practice.oxfam. org.uk/publications/quick-guide-to-gender-sensitive-indicators-312420   (last accessed April 2014), 3 pp.

Stating that 'using gender-sensitive indicators can help us to understand how changes in gender relations happen which enables more effective planning and delivery of future work', this extremely helpful and accessible short guide explains the different kinds of indicators used in different stages of a project cycle, sets out what is meant by 'gender-sensitive' indicators, and briefly describes how to develop gender-sensitive indicators for a project or programme.

Gender and Indicators: BRIDGE Cutting Edge Pack (2007), Brighton: Institute of Development Studies, www.bridge.ids.ac.uk/go/bridge-publications/cutting-edge-packs/gender-and-indicators/gender-and-indicators&langid=1 (last accessed April 2014)

Arguing that 'gender-sensitive indicators and other measurements of change are critical for building the case for taking gender (in)equality seriously, for enabling better planning and actions, and for holding institutions accountable for their commitments on gender ', this Cutting Edge Pack from BRIDGE contains an Overview Report, a Supporting Resources Collection, and a short briefing paper. The Overview Report defines gender-sensitive indicators and measurements of change, outlines their use, and follows with sections focusing on measuring in particular areas, such as gender-based violence, and the gender dimensions of poverty. It goes on to assess some international measures and indices, and concludes with a set of recommendations. The Supporting Resources is a wide-ranging collection of summaries and case studies of writings, tools, and initiatives relating to gender and indicators plus a list of organisations working on gender and indicators, as of 2007. The short briefing paper gives a succinct overview of gender and measuring change, followed by two case studies, one from the project level, the other from the international level.

Gender Indicators: What, Why and How? (n.d.), Justina Demetriades, prepared for the OECDDAC Network on Gender Equality, based on BRIDGE's Gender and Indicators Cutting Edge Pack 2007, www.oecd.org/social/gender-development/43041409.pdf (last accessed April 2014), 10 pp.

This short briefing paper focuses on the use of gender indicators as a way of measuring change, outlining what indicators are, and why we should develop gender indicators. It also addresses the often political issue of what we should be measuring, providing some broad principles that can be considered in making these decisions, as well as some questions donors can ask themselves when they are developing gender indicators. The document also offers examples of existing indicators, noting that they always need to be adapted to specific contexts.

Global gender indices

Gender Inequality Index, http://hdr.undp.org/en/statistics/gii

The Gender Inequality Index (GII) has been developed by the United Nations Development Programme (UNDP) as part of its work on monitoring human development (see the UNDP's annual Human Development Reports), alongside the Human Development Index, the Inequality Adjusted Human Development Index, and the Multi-dimensional Poverty Index. All seek to provide a human-centred assessment of development, rather than relying on purely national economic data. The GII replaces UNDP's previous gender indices, the Gender Development Index and the Gender Empowerment Index, and is a country-level measure of inequality between women and men in three areas; reproductive health, empowerment, and the labour market.

Gender Equality Index, http://eige.europa.eu/content/gender-equality-index

Created by the European Institute for Gender Equality, an independent agency of the European Union (EU), the Gender Equality Index was officially launched in 2013 and provides results for the EU overall, and for each Member State, giving a measure of how far (or close) each Member State was from achieving gender equality in 2010. Categories measured are work, money, knowledge, time, power, and health.

Global Gender Gap Index, World Economic Forum, www.weforum.org/issues/global-gender-gap

The Global Gender Gap Index was developed in 2006 and is published annually by the World Economic Forum (WEF). It calculates the national gender gaps of 136 countries on economic, political, and education- and health-based criteria. Unsurprisingly, the WEF makes an instrumentalist case for monitoring gender inequality, noting 'the strong correlation between a country's gender gap and its national competitiveness. Because women account for one-half of a country's potential talent base, a nation's competitiveness in the long term depends significantly on whether and how it educates and utilizes its women.'

Social Institutions and Gender Index, www.oecd.org/dev/poverty/theoecdsocialinstitutionsandgenderindex.htm#results2012

The Social Institutions and Gender Index (SIGI) is a measure of gender equality developed in 2009, based on the Organisation for European Co-operation and Development's Institutions and Development Database, and seeks to measure underlying discrimination against women in more than 100 countries. Rather than measuring gender inequality in areas such as education and employment, for example, the SIGI aims to quantify discriminatory social institutions, such as early marriage, discriminatory inheritance practices, violence against women, son bias, restrictions on access to public space, and restricted access to productive resources.

To Measure is to Know? A Comparative Analysis of Gender Indices, ISS Working Paper No. 2011–02 (2011), Irene Van Staveren, The Hague: Institute of Social Studies, www.indsocdev.org/resources/ISD%20Working%20Paper%202011-02.pdf (last accessed April 2014), also available at Review of Social Economy 71(3): 339–72

In this paper, the author uses a human development, or Capabilities, approach to compare and contrast a set of five, cross-country gender indices; the Gender Equality Index (created by the Institute of Social Development), the Gender Inequality Index (United Nations Development Programme), the Social Institutions and Gender Index (Organisation for European Co-operation and Development), the Global Gender Gap Index (World Economic Forum), and the Women's Economic Opportunities Index (Economic Intelligence Unit). The author concludes that the indices are 'clearly not interchangeable, and the selection of a particular gender index should be justified carefully to make its use in scholarly research and policy analysis meaningful', and to this end she provides three 'decision trees' to help in the choice of a suitable index for use by readers.

Standards and guidelines

Oxfam Minimum Standards for Gender in Emergencies (2013), Oxford: Oxfam International, http://policy-practice.oxfam.org.uk/publications/oxfam-mini-mum-standards-for-gender-in-emergencies-305867 (last accessed April 2014), 6 pp.

Developed in the first instance for Oxfam staff to ensure a consistent approach to promoting gender equality in Oxfam's humanitarian programming, these standards constitute a valuable tool for humanitarian practitioners across the sector. Intended to be referred to throughout the project cycle to inform planning; programme design and implementation; and monitoring, evaluation, accountability, and learning, the document sets out 16 minimum standards, plus a set of key actions necessary for the meeting of these standards.

Guidelines for Gender-based Violence Interventions in Humanitarian Settings: Focusing on Prevention of and Response to Sexual Violence in Emergencies (2005), Geneva: Inter-Agency Standing Committee, https://ochanet.unocha.org/p/Documents/GBV%20Guidelines%20(English).pdf (last accessed April 2014) 90 pp.

Prepared by the Inter-Agency Standing Committee (IASC), which is the body that co-ordinates both United Nations (UN) agencies and non-UN partners in humanitarian responses around the world, this set of Guidelines (also available in Arabic, Bahasa, French, and Spanish) aims to enable communities, governments, and humanitarian organisations to establish and implement a set of minimum interventions to prevent and respond to sexual violence during the early phase of an emergency. The multi-sectoral Action Sheets contained within the Guidelines provide a tool for implementing interventions in a range of sectors, including: Water and sanitation; Food security and nutrition; and Shelter and site planning and non-food items.

Ethical and Safety Recommendations for Researching, Documenting and Monitoring Sexual Violence in Emergencies (2007), Geneva: World Health Organization, www.who.int/gender/documents/OMS_Ethics&Safety10Aug07.pdf (last accessed April 2014), 33 pp.

The introductory section to this document states, 'In some emergency settings, simply participating in sexual violence inquiries can have serious, even life-threatening implications, not only for the participants themselves, but for the community and those involved in collecting information'. Rather than constituting a 'how to' methodological tool for conducting information collection into sexual violence, these recommendations focus on the ethical considerations involved. After a section on key concepts and definitions, the recommendations themselves are organised into eight thematic areas: Risks and benefits; Methodology; Referral services; Safety; Confidentiality; Informed consent; Information gathering team; and Children. An annex provides a useful list of recommended resources and further reading.

About the author

Liz Cooke is Assistant Editor of Gender and Development journal, Oxfam GB.

Oxfam GB is a development, relief, and campaigning organization that works with others to find lasting solutions to poverty and suffering around the world. Oxfam GB is a member of Oxfam International.

As part of its programme work, Oxfam undertakes research and documents its programme and humanitarian experience. This is disseminated through books, journals, policy papers, research reports, campaign reports, and other online products which are available for free download at: www.oxfam.org.uk/publications

www.oxfam.org.uk
Email: publish@oxfam.org.uk
Tel: +44 (0) 1865 473727

Oxfam House
John Smith Drive
Cowley
Oxford, OX4 2JY

The chapters in this book are available to download from the website:
www.oxfam.org.uk/publications

The *Working in Gender and Development series* brings together themed selections of the best articles from the journal *Gender & Development* and other Oxfam publications for development practitioners and policy makers, students, and academics. Titles in the series present the theory and practice of gender-oriented development in a way that records experience, describes good practice, and shares information about resources. Books in the series will contribute to and review current thinking on the gender dimensions of particular development and relief issues.

For further information on the journal please visit
www.genderanddevelopment.org
Other titles in the series include:
Gender-Based Violence
HIV and AIDS
Climate Change and Gender Justice
Gender and the Economic Crisis
Gender, Faith and Development